Memories

Memories

We write these lines...

to tell you...

MEMORIES

Willa Jean Johnson Cagle &
Mary Lucille Johnson Wilson

www.BluewaterPublications.com

TABLE OF CONTENTS

Acknowledgements

First of all, we wish to thank Cathy Cagle, Willa Jean's daughter, for all the many hours she spent at the computer, working tirelessly and never losing her cool with two old ladies who laughed and cried and lost all track of time. Of course it was no wonder, since their mother never believed in counting time. Cathy was not only instrumental in putting the paper into chapters and into some semblance of order; she also kept us on the right track when we seemed to be sliding off. She was always there with note pads, sharpened pencils, boxes of old pictures, and Kleenex, if needed, and was it ever needed! We even had a hard time finding a publisher, but once again, Cathy was right there, searching until we made the right choice.

We spent hours and hours looking at pictures and reading old letters and singing old songs. We looked up stories in order to verify facts, and even then some stories seemed to be somewhat colored, and we had to admit they might be folklore.

We wish to thank all our families for the generous allowance of their time. Anytime great grandchildren allow Mammas and Memes to have hours away from them telling stories, writing playfully, and crying, that is really a generous allowance!

We especially wish to thank James, Willa Jean's husband, for helping us to put this book together. He accomplished this feat by cooking, making gallons of coffee, bringing home take-outs, and just being there when we needed him.

And last, but not least, let us thank all our children, who have waited patiently all these years for us to come up with something that they might hold on to—a bit of themselves to hand down to their own children. So here's to Ralph, Denny, Carolyn, Cathy, Marilyn, as well as to Buddy's children—Janet, Jerry, Janie, Mary Jo, and to Robert's children-- Johnny and Jennifer. We love you and hope you will enjoy reading about the most precious mother in the world to us!

Prologue

"We write these lines to tell you" about the person who has made the most extraordinary impression upon our lives. From the time when we first heard the soft strums of the old guitar playing the tune of "My Little Girl" and Mother whispering softly about the "Wildwood Park" until the time we watched her last breaths so very close to the scenes she described in her song she sang to us, our lives were completely filled with wonder and amazement that one person could radiate such love. But she did and always had plenty to share with others. This song, written by Mother during the depression, reveals her deep love for "Dockie", our dad, and also shows how terribly broke they were. Mother may not have known much about poetic justice, but she used it quite successfully. We hope the readers will enjoy the song and the book, but most of all, we hope they will get a glimpse of one of the most unforgettable women that we have ever known—our precious mother.

We have so many memories to record and such a short time in which to record them. Over the years our children have asked us to jot down the little incidents that have made us the family that we are today, but memories seem to fade away when reality sets in, and instead of writing down what we recall, we begin reliving the past with laughter and with tears.

So here, in this little book, we (Willa Jean and Lucille) will take our children, our grandchildren, and our great-grandchildren back to their roots—that is, as far back as we can remember or can remember having been told. As much as possible, we plan to authenticate what we do not know first hand, but of course many of the facts are colored by having been told by slightly "prejudiced" kinfolk. One example of this coloring is the unfinished episode surrounding the grave of James Madison Allen Jackson Levi Roy Mason which we couldn't find on the route from Corinth to Shiloh. What a wonderful project this would be for one of our great-great grandchildren!

Our book is dedicated to the memory of our precious mother, Jeannie Veandra Mahatha Johnson Alexander, who lived a very short but extraordinary life, leaving a legacy which will live on for generations to come in the lives of her grandchildren and her great-grandchildren.

> "We look before and after,
> And pine for what is not;
> Our sincerest laughter
> With some pain is fraught;
> Our sweetest songs are those
> That tell of saddest thought."
> Percy B. Shelley

Our book will do just that...Hopefully; there will be enough laughter to counteract the tears; enough courage and honor to counteract the sorrow and pain. Throughout all the years, from the past with James Madison Allen Jackson Levi Roy Mason to the future with little Gavin Anderson Swint, this family will continue to make memories— memories that "My Little Girl" would be proud to share with "Dockie", the man of her dreams.

My Little Girl

I write these lines to tell you that I'm sorry I left
home,
Because I'm all alone.
Why did you let me roam?
Someone put the jinks on me, I'm up against it
strong.
I'm all out of luck - so I wrote this song.

Chorus: My little Girl: you know I love you—and I
long for you each day;
My little Girl, I'm dreaming of you, tho you're many
miles away;
I see the lane---down in the "Wildwood", where you
promised to be true;
My little Girl, I'm dreaming of you, and I'm coming
home to you.

The next verse, dear, is not complete, I cannot rhyme
the part—
that goes with aching heart—while I was never
smart;
But if some day I sell this tune, I'll marry you in
June.
If not, there'll be no honeymoon...
(Repeat Chorus)
> J.V.M. (1922)

Daddy 1922

Mother in Wildwood Park 1922

Daddy & Mother 1922

Chapter 1: Mason / Mahatha / Harbin Ancestry

How can we tell about ourselves and who we really are unless we tell about our own mother and who she actually was? The excitement in our own lives fades in comparison to hers. If only we had a small part of the courage and determination of "Miss Jeannie".. Yet she would be the first to say "Go to it, girls", so here it goes... Mother was born in Lawrence County, Tennessee, on August 12, 1903, and she died in Lauderdale County, Alabama, on September 5, 1955. She is buried next to her parents in Jones Hill Cemetery near Evergreen Estates in Florence, Alabama. Jeannie got most of her stamina and determination from her mother "Lou", whose own life was also filled with mystery and intrigue. We first met our grandmother, Mary Lucille Mason Mahatha, when we were about six and eight years old, respectively, and were visiting Alabama for the first time in our lives. Lou's jet black eyes seemed to stare right through us, and we had to admit we were a little frightened. She was of relatively short stature with high cheek bones and dark complexion. However, she must have been very attractive when she was younger because in her early fifties, when we first met her, we could feel the magnetism of her personality. Mamahatha, which was our name for her, was born February 8, 1886, to William Allen Mason and Nancy Margaret Kimbrell, of Lawrenceburg, Tennessee. Her grandfather was James Madison Allen Jackson Levi Roy Mason, a Cherokee Indian of the Echoa Tribe (the Bird Clan). He was born September 14, 1817, somewhere in the

Cumberland Mountains, in Tennessee. He was an Indian guide for the Confederate Army. He went by the name of James Lee Mason. There was one story about his being with his brothers Joseph and John in Oklahoma and being in a card game with a Choctaw Indian. They got into a fight and James Mason shot the Choctaw. He later hid out and his children brought him food. He died of measles after the Battle of Shiloh, on April 6, 1862, while serving as a guide for the Confederate Army. He was married to Louisa Hall and was buried somewhere between Shiloh and Corinth, Mississippi. We know very little about our Cherokee ancestors, but we do plan to continue our research about our family and will add to these notes as we find the information. Carolyn, Aunt Jo and Willa Jean visited the Archives Building in Lawrenceburg and were able to locate the gravesite of William Allen Mason, Lou's father and James Lee's son. He is buried in West Point, Tennessee, about ten miles from Lawrenceburg. Nancy Margaret Kimbrell, William Allen Mason's wife, is buried there also, and we are sure there are other Kimbrells, distant relatives of ours, buried there also. We plan to research the names of the Indians who escaped from the "Trail of Tears". We believe we will find some valuable information there. We do not, however, intend for this paper to be merely a listing of facts and dates. We plan to show our children, our grandchildren, and our great-grandchildren how they came to be just what they are--true Americans (mainly Republican Americans)--but we won't get into that just yet. If this project (book) does not get too overwhelming, we plan to delve into the lives of both sides of our families--- the Masons, the Kimbrells, the Johnsons, and the Dykes.

There are a number of interesting incidents to relate in all our families. Perhaps our children will become interested in this research project and add to the Mason family link here, or even to the Dyke link, which will show up, ironically, on the Johnson side of the family tree.

Mamahatha with family and banjo

We're not sure when Mamahatha first moved to Alabama. We would like to think it was when she was a little girl, since there are so many Masons who still live in Lauderdale County. We do know that at one time, as a little girl, she lived in Elgin, Alabama. However, Mother, her oldest child, was born in Giles County, Tennessee. There is quite a bit of intrigue here in keeping with the romantic personality of Mary Lou Mason. During our research in Tennessee, we found that Mary Lou Mason had married a mysterious Mr. E. M. Hardin on January 9, 1902.

The marriage was recorded in Lawrence County, Tennessee. The next year, she was married to

Mamahatha.

Will Mahatha on June 1, 1903, in Center Star, Lauderdale County, Alabama. Her oldest daughter, Jeannie, was born

August 12, 1903. There was no record of the first marriage in the family Bible, and the date of the last marriage was incorrectly recorded on Mamahatha's tombstone as 1901. This mistake cannot be contributed to Mamahatha since the tombstone was erected after her death. Poptoe (as we called Will Mahatha) was a handsome person of relatively small stature and a quiet personality. He was from a large family (also with Indian heritage) with several brothers and sisters. One brother was John and another one was Jack. Both married young ladies named Emma; so we called them Aunt Emma John and Aunt Emma Jack. Since Poptoe was also of Cherokee Indian lineage with an Irish mixture, we felt closeness to him. We remember once after we moved to Alabama, however, that Mother became angry at Poptoe for scolding Robert, and she comforted Robert by saying, "He's not your real Grandaddy, anyway." At the time, we only thought she meant Grandaddy Johnson was our real Grandaddy, since we had always been so close to the Johnsons, but now we know what she meant, and that she had known all along that she was different from the rest of her siblings. How we wish she could have talked to us about this!

During our recent research concerning the mysterious disappearance of E.M. Hardin soon after his marriage to Lou Mason, we found that there had been animosity between Lou's father and Mr. Hardin, and that he was afraid of Lou's father. No one knows what happened to him, but, later, at a luncheon we had with our cousins, Louise White Tuberville and Helen White Quinn, daughters of Aunt Beatrice, Mother's sister, we were told that Lou's dad had given him a certain time to leave the country. Our cousins had known about Lou's marriage to E.M. since they were children and they knew that Mother was his child and therefore we were only "half" cousins to them, but they were told to "never" tell Jean's children. So this marriage was kept a deep dark secret from us until we were adults. Mother knew, of course, but we don't think Daddy ever did. We still only see romance and intrigue in the story and can't understand why anyone would not want to look long and hard for the story about the mysterious E.M. Hardin who was also part of our Cherokee Indian heritage. Someone has said that Hardin's disappearance was due to his fear of Lou's father, who had given him a certain time to leave the country. No one seems to know what happened to him. There is no record of him after Jeannie's birth.

Lou had two sisters and two brothers by her natural mother, who later died. Her father married again and had a number of children, many of whom settled in and around Anderson, Alabama. Mamahatha was only about 3/4 Indian, but she seemed totally "Cherokee!" She believed in chants, cards, spells, you name it! She could "witch" for money or for water with a "witching stick." How we loved to go out in the woods with Mamahatha and her magic stick. It would take an abrupt, brisk twist toward the ground, and she would say, "There it is, start digging", and we dug! We don't remember getting any money, but we really had a lot of fun! Children today don't have the opportunity to explore in magic woods the way we did, both in Seymour woods in Tennessee with mother, and then later in Alabama woods with Mamahatha. It seems like a twist in fate that while both these wonderful women taught us so much about the joys of outdoor living, now they are both buried side by side in the same wooded area where Mamahatha's woodland excursions took place in the quiet, peaceful section of Lauderdale County called Evergreen Estates. Please forgive us for digressing, but memories do get tangled in reality. But back to normality, the first thing Lou did when she got up in the morning was "cut" her cards to see what kind of day she would have and "Woe unto you!" if that old black jack of spades showed up on the top of the deck. Her black eyes would glitter, and we would look for a place to hide! She would cut those cards again and pick up another to go with it, and she really knew what she was doing. She could cap that off by reading coffee grounds. She would not like today's brewed coffee! She boiled her coffee in a pot and let the grounds settle in the bottom of the cup. Then she turned the cup over and let the grounds settle more. Then the route took shape. By that time, you knew what kind of a day you would have—a magical one! This was a whole new world for us.

We have very little knowledge about the family life of Mother's family. We do know Poptoe sharecropped at 4-Mile Branch and did not interact with many people socially. Since both Mamahatha and Poptoe were half or quarter Indian, we suppose there were prejudices involved, but if there were, Mother never mentioned them to us. They seemed to have lived normal lives with simple but well rounded meals. Mother and her brother and sisters attended church. We suppose the community was quite surprised to see such beautiful young people emerge from this unique family.

Our mother, Jeannie Veandra Mahatha, was the oldest of Lou's four children: Beatrice (husband Van C.

White), Walter (who married Barbara Robinson), and Elise (husband W. C. Berry). Mother loved her family dearly, but never seemed to really fit in. Her wants and needs were quite different from those of her sisters and her brother. From a very early age, she loved to "make music." Mamahatha was also musically inclined and built her own

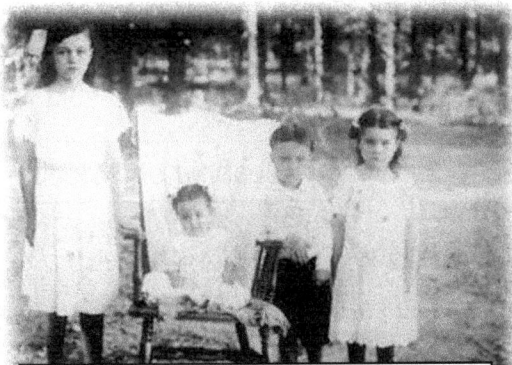

Jeannie, Elise, Walter, Beatrice

"music box" (similar to today's dulcimer). Undoubtedly, as a young lady, Lou Mason had music on her mind. These strains of musical tendencies have continued on into the present generations.

Her granddaughter Marilyn Cagle McWilliams, received a bachelor's degree in music from the University of North Alabama, the very center of learning where Jeannie was in her early life.

Mamahatha & children

13

Other children have followed in her footsteps. Carolyn, Cathy, and Marilyn, Willa Jean's daughters, performed as a trio at many weddings, and Sara Elizabeth, Lucille's great-granddaughter is a talented singer. Lou often dressed flamboyantly, wearing flashing satin dresses with matching make-up and jewelry. To us, her grandchildren, she looked very much like an Indian princess. She loved to listen to gospel singing on the radio, especially on Saturday nights with Roy Acuff

Jeannie on wheels.

and "The Great Speckled Bird"! We would go to sleep listening to the strumming of the musical instruments and Mamahatha's feet keeping time to the music. She enjoyed all country blue grass, but especially quartet, trios and other harmonies. She really liked the rhythm of square dancing which she joined in with occasionally. Mamahatha's hair was completely unique. It was always short, and most of the time was in pin-curls.

As a small child, Mother loved to play on Lou's

Beatrice & Jeannie

The Mahatha Sisters

14

musical instruments, and her mother later bought her an organ, which became her most precious possession. She spent many hours practicing on this instrument, and as a teenager, was involved in the music ministry at Goodsprings Cumberland Presbyterian Church at Elgin. Jeannie was also a gifted singer and attended many all-day singings during this time of her life. She never tired of this type of music and continued her enthusiasm for gospel singing until her death. This love of gospel music can be seen in her grandsons, Denny and Ralph, who are now personal friends of Ben Speer, a famous gospel singer.

Jeannie at 18 yrs.

While Mother was still a teenager, her family was living at "4-Mile Branch", a small community which is now known as Belle Meade subdivision where Helen B, Aunt B's daughter lived until her death in 2005 and not far at all from where both Mother and Mamahatha are buried in Jones Cemetery at Evergreen Estates. This location is just across the highway from where Willa Jean's granddaughter Caryn now lives in Kendale Gardens. Caryn, who has the same sparkling blue eyes and black hair as Mother, could easily pass as Miss Jeannie's daughter rather than her great-granddaughter.

Our mother's life was filled with bitter disappointments, but somehow she always seemed to overcome these tragedies. We don't know where mother attended high school, but it was either Lauderdale County High, or she was self-taught. Regardless, she was admitted to Florence State Normal College for Teachers in 1922 and was attending there when she met "Dock", William Cooley Ellis Johnson, who was working on the construction of Lee Highway, which runs through Rogersville today, and is now called Lee Street. Dock also helped build the old Shoals Creek Bridge, which has now been replaced by a more modern structure. We're not sure if it was "love at first sight", but Daddy had never been interested in "girls" before. He was absolutely smitten by this lovely creature who was not only beautiful, but also talented. Daddy loved music, also, but his best was singing "Coming Around the Mountain," or "How Come There a Cabbage Head?"

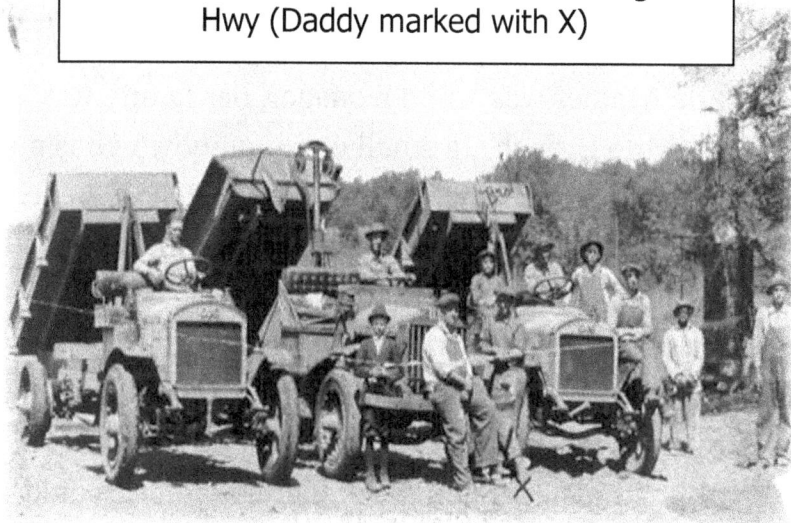

Construction crew from Knoxville building Lee Hwy (Daddy marked with X)

Chapter 2: Johnson / Dykes Ancestry

Dock was from a large family in Knoxville and Seymour, Tennessee. He had nine sisters and two brothers. The boys were naturally extremely spoiled, and the girls thought the boys could do no wrong. None of the Johnsons thought anyone was good enough for their boys, so those who married did so very late in life. Even the Johnson girls had to leave home to meet their future spouses. Aunt Kate, who married H.A. Burch, Superintendent of Education in Tupelo, Mississippi, and Aunt Mildred, who married Herschel Wheeler, Deputy Sheriff in Corinth, Mississippi, both eloped. The Johnson family had lived in Seymour, the northeastern section of Tennessee, for centuries with ancestors dating back to before the Civil War. Aunt Kate declared we are in Andrew Johnson's family tree, and while we have not yet documented that fact, it would be an interesting project for our grandchildren to pursue. Our grandfather's name has quite a pseudo-history in itself. It seems that in eastern Tennessee in November and December of 1863, Ambrose E. Burnside, Major General in the Union Army, led a campaign through Knoxville, killing cattle and taking as much other food as possible. Our great-grandmother asked that he spare her cow since she was expecting a child, and said if he would do so she would name her child Burnside after him. This she did, and so our grandfather was named Newman Burnside.

We know little about the Dykes side of our kinfolk, but here we also are hoping our children and grandchildren will continue our study. According to Jim Dykes, Uncle Bob Dykes' son who is a reporter for the Knoxville Journal, there could be Cherokee blood on the Johnson side of our family also. (See Appendix) It seems almost unbelievable that our frail little "Mary Elizabeth" grandmother, who was so quiet and soft-spoken, could have somehow been even distantly related to our vivacious and active little "Mary Lou" grandmother on the Mason side.

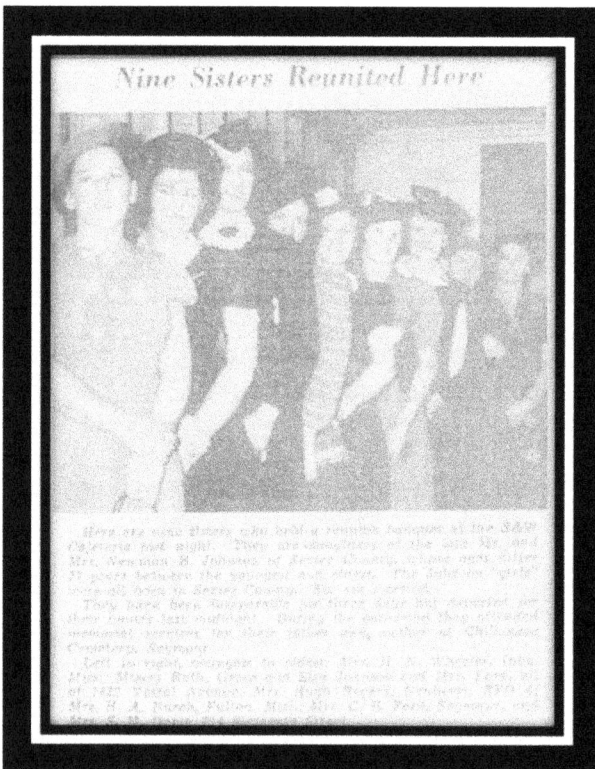

Our dad, William Cooley Ellis (Dock), was the middle son and the fourth child of Newman Burnside Johnson of Seymour County and Mary Elizabeth Dykes of Boyd's Creek, Tennessee. His siblings were Elmer Ernest (wife Maude), Daisy (husband Stuart Davis), Ida (husband Cliff Ford), Ina (husband Hugh Rogers), Kathryn (husband H.A. Burch), Pearl (husband "Mutt" Ford), Grace, Elsie, Ruth, Paul (wife Cleo), and Mildred (husband Herschel Wheeler).

Chapter 3: William Cooley Ellis Johnson Family Begins

Daddy was twenty-six when he first met Mother. She was a student at Florence Normal Teacher's College and lived in Ingram's Crossroads, which is now known as Elgin, Alabama. Mother never enjoyed working on a farm nor doing farm work. She loved playing her organ and could play for hours at a time. Her parents saw her potential for higher education and allowed her to enter Florence State Normal School for

Jeannie at 19 yrs.

Dockie dressed up.

Teachers. Dad had moved to Alabama with his older brother's construction company to work on the building of Lee Highway and Shoal Creek Bridge.

Dock & Jeannie.

While working at Elgin, he went up to a house for a drink of water and met a vision of loveliness named Jeannie Mahatha, who was not only beautiful, but also

Dock & Jeannie's first hut.

available. They seemed to enjoy the same things—both loved music and laughter. So after about a year of courtship, they were married (without his sisters' permission) at Ingram's Crossroads on November 11, 1922.

When they began their married life, Daddy was a

Mary Lucille, Buddy & Mother.

truck driver and Mother was a housewife. At this time, she never dreamed she would soon be living in Knoxville and certainly never dreamed she would be the mother of four children. Rather, her dreams had been to be a great pianist or a

teacher of music or elocution. The latter two dreams she pursued for the rest of her life, even while becoming one of the world's most loved mothers. Since Dock couldn't go back to Knoxville until the construction on Lee Highway was completed, he and his new bride lived in a tiny hut at first (see picture), then "roomed" with Turner Lindsey in Rogersville. Jeannie must have dropped out of school after her marriage, for Buddy was

Jeannie, Mary Lucille & Buddy

born on January 25, 1924, two years after their nuptials. Their first home was the Turner Lindsey house in Rogersville. (Forty-two years later, as a new bride, Cathy, Jeannie and Dock's granddaughter moved into Turner Lindsey's house in Rogersville which was also her first home.) It was in this home that Elmer Ellis (Buddy) Johnson was born. He seemed a healthy, handsome, and outgoing young lad. Two years later, on November 7, 1925, Mary Lucille, named for both her grandmothers, was born. There is a little question about the location of Mary Lucille's birth. Since Lou was a mid-wife, there was a possibility that the birth was never recorded. Aunt Elise later told us she was there when Mary Lucille was born and that Mamahatha always sent in a record when she helped to deliver a child.

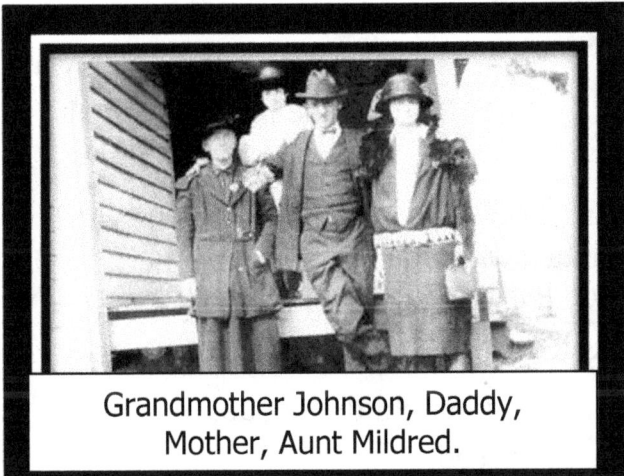

Grandmother Johnson, Daddy, Mother, Aunt Mildred.

Aunt E had a picture showing Mary Lucille and the home in which she was born. She said the home was close to the line between Lauderdale and Limestone County. Regardless of the exact location, we know that Jeannie and Dock's second child was a beautiful little girl destined to write her memoir about just this very thing. When living in

Knoxville, she was called Mary because of her daddy's mother, and when in Alabama, she was called Lucille because of Mary Lou (Lucille) her mother's mother. So one can see that at a very early age she was made extremely conscience of her heritage and of the wide gap between the two families. Lucille had an abundance of blonde curls to complement her fair complexion, and the two children won a great number of compliments because of their beauty. Their appearance, however, was not what was so unusual about the children; it was their behavior which was unique in children that young.

Doc & Jeannie hunting with Elise in Wildwood Park.

Jeannie began early training her children to be polite, to sing, and to listen. She also read to them when they were very young. Later, none of her children could remember when they first learned to read.

Chapter 4: Baker Avenue House

When work on Highway 72 in North Alabama was completed, the new Johnson family of four packed up their earthly belongings and moved to Knoxville, Daddy's hometown. Their first home was 637 Baker Avenue. It was here that Willa Jean, their third child (Wednesday's child), was born at 3:15 a.m., October 28, 1927. By this time, the country was on the brink of the Great

November 1927 – Buddy, Lucille & Willa Jean – Baker Avenue House.

Depression, and things were about to change drastically, not only for the country but for the Johnson family also.

Lucille does not recall much about this time with her baby sister or her house--after all, she was only twenty-three months old, but she clearly remembers playing with little cars and trucks in the backyard.

November 1927 – Buddy, Lucille & Willa Jean – Baker Avenue House.

Actually, she still has one of the little red trucks with which she and "Bubba" played together for hours. Once while the

woman who was staying with Mother was hanging out clothes on the line, the children tried to use the sheets as tents and put their muddy hands on them. They didn't get a spanking, but they were roundly scolded. When Willa Jean was born, Mary Evelyn, Aunt Id's and Uncle Cliff's daughter was born two days earlier. She was tiny and fragile while Willa Jean was robust and healthy. The four Johnson sisters who were still living at home took turns taking care of the new moms and their babies. Just a little resentment of the Alabama mom could be seen as the Johnson girls had to take care of an outsider. In time the resentment diminished when they realized that the children were also Johnson children and that Jeannie was a devoted wife to their beloved Dock.

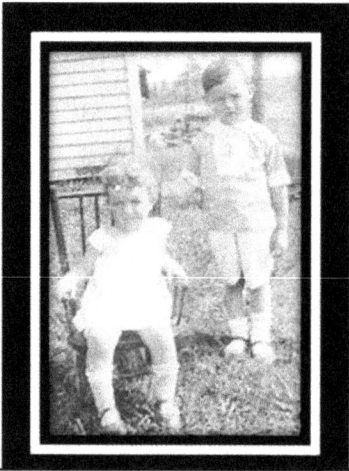

November 1927 – Buddy & Lucille – Baker Avenue House

By the close of the 1920's, dark clouds were beginning to roll over the country. Families, who had always seemed secure, suddenly lost all they had. Many men could not take the pressure and committed suicide. Others turned to drink. Almost all lost their jobs, their homes, even their self-respect. Our daddy was no exception. If he owned the house on Baker Avenue, he lost it. He also lost his job. He always knew, however, that he could go home again, back to Seymour, Tennessee, the place that his dad and mom lived. So this is the place to which he now turned.

Chapter 5: House on the Hill - 1929

Uncle Ern, Daddy's oldest brother, had a house just right for us, one we immediately thought of as "our house on the hill." It was a beautiful home out in the country in Seymour overlooking the Chilhowee Cemetery and the Chilhowee Institute (our first school). It was in this home that Mother had her last baby, Robert Henry, born December 25, 1929—our Christmas baby. He was named for two Dykes—our great uncles Robert Dykes, a Baptist preacher, and Henry, his brother, a blind boot-legger. On Christmas Eve, the night Robert was

Uncle Robert Dykes (Baptist Preacher).

born, we had a deep snow which came to Daddy's and Uncle Cliff's knees when they carried us on their backs down to Grandpa's house and put us in bed with our two aunts (Aunt Grace and Aunt Elsie) because it was so cold. We left

House on the Hill.

our house crying because our dolls wouldn't cry, and Mother's doll cried. Sister's doll's hair was painted on its head. Bubba got a pretty red sled. We never knew just how Bubba felt about the excitement of this Christmas Day. He was always quiet and smiling. He must have known, even then, that we should enjoy every moment that we were all together. But the two rambunctious little girls, unknowingly, rushed blindly into the future with laughter bubbling and long curls flying. The hill made a perfect place to ride Bubba's sled in the snow—all the way down to Grandpa's house. While

Smoky Mountain Trip.

we were too young to appreciate such things as a view, the view from the house on the hill was, and still is, spectacular. It overlooks the Chilhowee Cemetery and faces the foothills of the Great Smoky Mountains. While we didn't call them that, nor did we try to

Johnson Cousins: 1st row: Hughella, Mary Evelyn, Willa Jean, 2nd row: Mary Lucille, Bill, Buddy Johnson, 3rd row: Dorothy, Margaret, Joe, 4th row: Kathryn, Ella Ree, Murelle, Elizabeth holding Jack, Ray, Buddy Davis.

describe their beauty, we pretended one cloud belonged to Sister and one to Willa Jean. We saw all sorts of "things" up there. They are still there if one only takes the time and uses the vision of a child's eyes to see.

In the spring, while Robert was still a tiny baby, Willa Jean got him off the bed, brought him to the front porch carrying him out by the neck and said, "See what a beautiful baby! He's my little Robbie Neal." This old house had an attic which was filled with trunks. Some were "no, no's" for us, but some were allowed to be explored. One in particular, we remember, was filled with old baby clothes and shoes. They probably belonged to Aunt Maude and Ella Ree, but we played with them for hours. We remember one pair of baby shoes with high tops and purple buttons. Later, Mother sang a song to us, "Put My Little Shoes Away", and we always thought of those shoes. (see appendix)

Our memories become blurred about this time when we try to recall exact incidents. Most of all we recall happy memories: running down the hill to Grandpa and Grandma's house, eating apples from the apple orchard, climbing in the hack, smelling the clothes hanging on the line, swinging on the rope swing in the front yard. Grandpa also had a cistern, and he let us yell down in it. It was for catching rainwater. He had a buggy and a hack. Lucille was scared of him (he had a ruddy complexion, a handlebar mustache, a gruff voice, but was really like a teddy bear). Willa Jean was more afraid of Grandma (she was tiny and fragile, but Willa Jean thought she was sad looking and was always afraid she would die). At the time we did not know that Grandma had consumption (tuberculosis). Willa Jean recalls the time that Grandpa let us help him sharpen his tools on the grinder in his shed. She missed the grinder and cut her finger instead. He was so kind and careful with her hand. We also used to watch Aunt Elsie peel apples from the orchard. She would start at the top and peel all around each apple without breaking the peel! She then divided the apples from the peelings to make jelly from one and apple butter from the other. Grandpa and Grandma always had cows and chickens, and the kitchen always smelled like fried chicken and apple pie. We can't remember their having pigs, but they must have. They lowered their butter and milk in containers into the cistern which was just off the back porch. The old Johnson homeplace is still standing today (2004); but the orchard is gone as well as the big oak trees, the cistern, and the old hack. The wonderful memories, however, remain and come flooding back each trip we make to Seymour and to the old house on the hill.

We always enjoyed going to our Johnson grandparents and aunts' home. They always kept it clean and beautifully organized but never too daunting to make us feel uncomfortable. They always spoke to us children as adults. Our grandmother was bedfast from 1929 until she died in 1934. At the time of her death, Aunts Grace, Ruth, Elsie and Mildred were all living at

Daddy & kids with car
1929

home. Those aunts were always referred to as simply "the girls". They told us that Grandma had gone to the Knoxville Market one bad, rainy day, to sell vegetables, eggs, and milk, and she had stayed wet all day. From that experience, she developed a severe cold that was never cured, and she later died of tuberculosis. Grandpa had built her a special sun room on the side of the house, enclosing part of the porch with screens and windows. The daughters took such wonderful, loving care of her. We really do not remember seeing her out of bed. Aunt Elsie contracted TB from Grandma and died in 1944 at the age of 41. The Johnsons were a very loving family.

Chapter 6: The Pitner House

Ironically as our nation grew deeper and deeper into poverty and our own family lost more and more materially, our familial love grew stronger, and as children we were happier than ever. We had to move from our beautiful home on the hill to the Pitner House, a small little cottage around the curve in the woods. We also now shared the love of our mom and dad who allowed us to have nine dogs at one time (Queen and her seven puppies along with her husband Spot #1). See picture.

The most fascinating thing about our Pitner House was the magic woods outside the back door which led to, of all places, Grandpa and Grandma's house in another direction. But

Buddy, Willa Jean, Robert & Lucille with Old Queen, Spot #1 and puppies.

before one could get there, he had to go through the forest which was covered with moss and ferns. Mother would play with us there for hours, with Robert and Buddy being the cowboys on sticks, and Lucille and Willa Jean playing house on the moss. Mother would bring out her sewing and writing and would stay with us all day. She always had the time to take up with us. Willa Jean remembers once getting lost in those magic woods. She decided to go see Grandpa all by herself and after walking for quite a while, she lay down by the path and went to sleep. It was quite a while before they found her, and things were not so pleasant for her for a while thereafter. There was also another incident that happened on the other side of the woods when Buddy and Lucille were in school. Mother was picking blackberries by the old oak tree (there's a story here too about the old oak tree, we'll get to that later), and she told Willa Jean to take care of Robert. They were playing by the old oak tree. He wet his diaper so Willa Jean took care of him by taking it off. They wandered on down the hill to the Seymour Elementary School where the two very brilliant older brother and sister, Buddy and Lucille, ages 5 and 7, and in grades 3 and 5, were in school. Willa Jean told the teacher that Robert would be happy to recite for her too, and he did--he also streaked! Mother was furious!! Oh, well, so much for happy memories.

And now the other old oak tree story—The highlight of our day was meeting our daddy at the old oak tree, which was about half way down the road from our house to the old town of Seymour. Daddy would come around the curve, and we would all sing, "Here comes Daddy, a rippin' around- a rippin around- a rippin around, here comes Daddy a rippin' around." He would grab each one of us up and swing us around. We can still see him now. He always wore a cap (like today's golf cap), and he was skinny as could be, even though that was the name he gave to Mother. We all had nicknames. Elmer was Bubba, Mary Lucille-Sister, Willa Jean-Wooley, and Robert-Bobby (or by Willa Jean Robbie Neal).

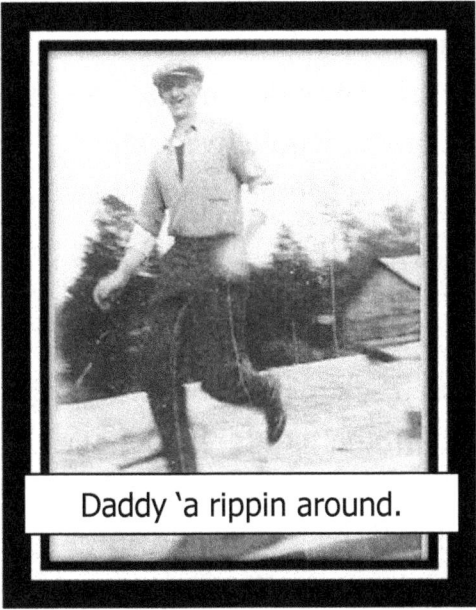
Daddy 'a rippin around.

We all loved school and were always anxious to go. Perhaps we took this love of learning from our mother who studied her entire life. She filled our young lives with love for books, newspapers, and poetry. We can remember climbing in her lap to hear bedtime stories every night until we were dangling off her lap. We don't know when we first began to read, but Buddy started to school at a very early age (about 4 years old, we believe).

Sister cried every day because she couldn't go with him; so just as soon as she could, they let her enter first grade also at age 4. We remember at the school they gave us intelligence tests and asked if there were any other little "Johnsons" at home they could test. And so they did!

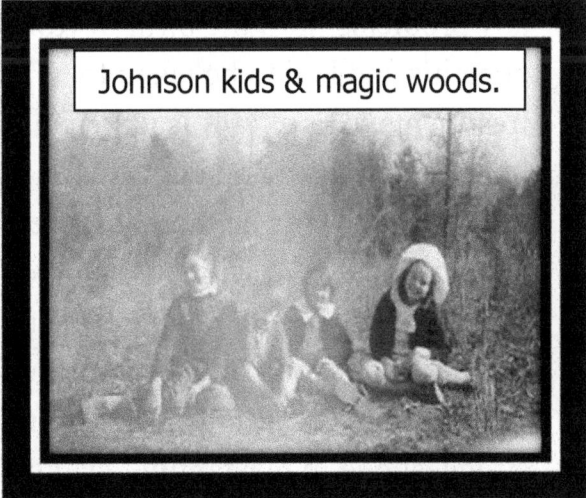
Johnson kids & magic woods.

Willa Jean started to school at age 4 also. Sister was promoted to grade 3 at 5 years of age; so we were quite a bit younger than other children in our classes. Sometimes this worked out well, but at other times, it was a detriment. Some children could be cruel, but on the whole, we really didn't mind since we loved to learn, and Mother was always there when we came home to ask us all about what we had accomplished. Sometimes bad weather and sickness kept us home, but we continued to study around an old brown library table. One day Bubba missed school, and Sister told the teacher he had to stay home so Mother could wash his overalls. He only had one pair that fit him. We're sure the teachers' appreciated our honesty! All the teachers loved Bubba so much (but so did everybody else). We never remember Bubba having any hard feelings toward anyone—never a fight nor an argument. He was very, very sweet. Our dear baby brother, however, was different, but still a "good" brother. We loved him and petted him all his life. Mother had RH negative blood which had not caused any problems until the birth of Robert. He was born with hepatitis and had to be taken to Knoxville Hospital for treatments. His skin was quite pallid, and we made no bones about his being our "pet" in the family. If things didn't go his way, he merely started to gag and said, "I'm choking", and everything would be forgiven. Actually, we can't remember ever having had any serious quarrels. Mother and Daddy loved each other and showed their love to us in so many little ways. Mother was probably the strongest one in our family. Daddy left early every morning for work and was late coming in so Mother had to care for our every need, and she was up for the task.

There are lasting memories of the Pitner House itself. It was picturesque, set back in a wooded area, surrounded by pines with mossy banks and wild flowers. It seemed to become a part of the natural background. The old house had never been painted and was covered with wood shingles. We didn't mind at all moving there because it had always seemed a part of the magic woods which surrounded it. Never mind that all the rooms leaked! The ping ping of the drips only added to the music made by Mother's imaginary piano. The house had two bedrooms. The beds were filled with straw ticks which we children got to "fluff" every day. At the time, we didn't realize the need for this labor! Mother made it seem like play. We girls slept on one bed and Robert and Buddy on the other. We don't recall ever having seen our parents in bed together. Daddy was always up and busy by the time we were out of bed. Our parents were very particular with their personal habits, and we children remained quite innocent throughout our childhood. We were a very loving family and went through the ritual of "Goodnight Daddy, Goodnight, Mother," etc....down through the family. That was why we found it so heartbreakingly amusing a few years later when we saw the same thing played out on a television series - "The Walton's".

Money certainly cannot buy happiness, and while our parents' lives were cut tragically short, they were filled with much happiness. Our parents never even hinted that we had to move from the very comfortable house on the hill to this cottage in the woods for financial reasons. Ironically, along with the larger house, went our one cow which had furnished us a tremendous amount of nourishment. This meant that Daddy had to work even longer hours, and Mother had to pick more berries and try to have a garden. She was never successful with this arrangement. Regardless of what else she had, Mother always had a semblance of a piano to brighten up our lives, even though at this time there were no students for piano lessons. As a matter of fact, her piano was made out of a long strip of cardboard with keys drawn on top. This board was placed on our library table, and Mother "played" the piano as we sang. No wonder our imaginations could work overtime. The love for music, reading, and books started during these years. Even though we did not have a piano, Mother would sing to us and with us. She had her own quartet. Bubba sang bass, Willa Jean sang alto, Sister sang tenor, and Bobby sang the melody if possible. We sang such classic American songs as: "Wait for the Wagon," "Camptown Races," and "She'll be Coming Round the Mountain". (See appendix) Mother read to us everyday some of the traditional, classic children's stories from a big thick book she had had in school. Willa Jean's favorite was the one about the prince who was an ugly frog and the princess who loved him anyway. He turned into a handsome prince, and they lived happily ever after. She used to follow Mother's finger along as she read from the book. We children got to take turns sitting in Mother's lap while she read aloud to us. We never grew too old for this habit. The rest of us gathered as closely around as possible. Mother put such emotion into her reading that one could actually feel what the characters were feeling! When she said, "Boo," we all jumped!! Later, we followed Mother as she read from books and newspapers so when we started to school, we couldn't remember when nor how we had learned to read. Years later, when Willa Jean taught first grade at Whitehead School in Lauderdale County in the 1950's, she had to teach her students to read phonetically. She had to learn this technique at home herself since she had never learned how to really use this method. She said she used to pray every night that her students would learn to read, and somehow they must have since years later she taught the same group in twelfth grade at Lauderdale County High School.

Mother not only sang folk songs, she made up her own songs as she went along. We recall in particular "My Little Girl" which is included in our prologue, and which we hope our own grandchildren will sing to their grandchildren someday. Sister recalls Mother singing "Stars Fell on Alabama Last Night" because she was so homesick for Alabama. She had not been home since 1926—the year Sister was one year old. We can't prove that Mother wrote this song, but we had no radio or any other type of communication so we don't know where she could have learned all the words and the tune. She was very talented writing music as well as in singing. She sent many of her original tunes to Nashville for copyrighting, but they were never returned. Mother must have been extremely homesick for Alabama about this time of her life. She spent hours strumming her guitar and singing some of the saddest songs: "Knoxville Girl"; "Little Mary Phagen"; "The Sandstorm Cave"; and the others she would make up as she went along. While these songs might have seemed unusual bedtime songs for some children, we all listened intently, and Daddy would chime in with his "Cabbage Head" or "Going Around the Mountain" then all would be just fine again. While Mother never forced us to participate in her singing, it seemed to come naturally, so by the time we were four or five years old, we were beginning to harmonize with her. She didn't have a piano at this time so she would strum a string on her guitar and say, "This is your pitch, Sister," or "this is your pitch, Willa Jean." She even gave Buddy his bass pitch, and away we would go. The Johnson girls, on the other hand, always had a piano, and we were always welcome to use it when we were visiting. So between the cardboard keyboard, the guitar, and the borrowed piano, we were blessed with musical instruments.

Mother also wrote short plays and readings which we recited at special events before we started to school and while we were in lower elementary school. Aunt Grace recalled taking us to Chilhowee Institute, where she taught elementary school, to recite selections for her Christmas program. The Johnson girls were also interested in our education and encouraged us to read and "recite" at every opportunity. Some recitations we made for Aunt Grace, an elementary school teacher, when we were four and six years old are included in the appendix of this book.

Our mother was a wonderful seamstress, even though she did not have a sewing machine. She was before her time in thinking of new and original articles of clothing to

Robert & Willa Jean

make. While we were living at the Pitner House, we remember one outfit--a pretty light orchid color checked chiffon dress which she made for our new cousin, Lady Ruth Burch, in about 1934. To decorate the hanger for the dress, Mother took a branch from a tree, cut it for a dress hanger, wrapped it in the material of the dress, tacked it with white embroidery thread, and made a loop to hang it from the wall. The little dress set was so outstanding and so pretty on Lady Ruth! (Years later, Lady Ruth won the title of Miss Hot Springs, Arkansas, but not in that dress.) Mother took pictures of Shirley Temple dolls and made outfits like hers without a pattern. She made bows for our hair and bloomers down to the knees to match. She also made clothes for our dolls.

We also had second and third cousins in Seymour with whom we spent hours playing. The Pitner's lived on a large farm down the hill from our Pitner house. We loved to visit with Joy and Loy, Ray and Faye, and their deformed sister Odessa, even though we were deadly afraid of her.

Mother & children at Pitner House.

We remember once the youngest set of twins set the house on fire at Christmas by dropping a candle on the Christmas tree, totally destroying the home, though no lives were lost. Odessa could not talk, but her hands could tell you plenty; so we had to stay out of the way of those hands. We loved playing in the silo and probably lived dangerously so many times without realizing what we were doing—but, oh, the joy of life in the country in the 1930's. The air was so pure, and we were all so happy and seemingly unaware of the gloomy depression which was looming over us.

While most families might have used food as a top priority in their conversations around the family table, we don't recall this subject coming up as a serious matter of concern. Daddy used to come around the old oak tree with a bag of flour over his shoulder, and Mother would come in from the berry patch with a gallon of blackberries, but we never seemed to worry about where the next meals would come from. Mother made large, good biscuits and gravy, and while there was not always sugar for the blackberries, they were okay with the biscuits, and Daddy taught us how to make "soakee" by soaking those delicious biscuits in coffee. (We were all coffee drinkers. No one had told our parents coffee was not good for children.) We were all in this together for the long haul. The main meat in our family meals was chicken, which we raised ourselves. Mother was a master at frying chicken, but she did not believe in spending hours in the kitchen. She preferred frying foods because that was faster. She made really good tea cakes, and she often made them and brought them to our play houses. We never had white beans or pinto beans. They took too long to cook, and she would not stay in the kitchen that long. She made excellent fried potatoes, battered like steak, and corn bread fritters, and as Sister keeps reminding me, good, good tea cakes. Everyday was interesting in our young lives. Mother devoted herself to us and seemed to enjoy being with us while Daddy had to work. We played with our toys and also made up games to play. We played "Annie Over" by tossing a ball over the house; we also played tag, "Red Rover," jumped rope for hours, and sang in harmony.

Knoxville, Tennessee, had very cold winters in the 1930's. We wore heavy underwear and we girls wore long cotton stockings from October until April. At that time girls did not wear slacks or jeans; both boys and girls wore flannel shirts or tops and lots of sweaters. The boys wore caps with flaps over the ears (called skull caps). We girls covered our heads with toboggans to keep us warm. The nights were very cold. Mother and Daddy would heat irons and wrap them in lots of cloths and put to our feet in bed. We always had a wood stove in our living (family) room and a large wood burning cook stove in the kitchen to heat the house, but all fires were out by bedtime. Daddy was up early every morning to build fires in both stoves, and then Mother got up and cooked a good breakfast. She made large biscuits every morning. We children would call from our bedroom, "Can I get up?" When the house was warm, the answer would be, "You can get up now." It was always pleasant to see smiling parents when you get up and to feel loved. We were ready to face the day. There were days when we all got corrected, and then we got a whipping with a "little" peach tree limb; we all got an equal dose. Mother would say, "I don't want to show partiality," so she gave us all a touch of the peach tree limb. Our corrections were usually on wash days. She hated to wash clothes because you had to rub them on a rub board, and we had to carry tubs of water.

While most of the time the Dock Johnson family was happy at the Pitner House (at least the children thought they all were), not all things were bright and cheerful. Daddy's younger brother, Paul, was quite a rake and a daredevil when he was drinking, which was quite often in those days. He was a teenager at that time. One day he decided since Dock was away at work, he would ride his horse right through our living room just to show us that he could do it. He had not counted on the Alabama girl's courage. It didn't take Mother but a few minutes to send both Uncle Paul and his horse riding back down the hill to Grandpa's house in a hurry. We don't think Mother ever told Daddy about this episode.

Chapter 7: Mad Dog House

As jobs grew more scarce and the country fell deeply into debt, Daddy became more restless and insecure.

Robert (Robby-Neal)

He didn't want to move back to Knoxville, but he had to find work to provide for his family. We moved to what our family called the Mad Dog House which was closer to the new highway in Seymour and presumably closer to his new work. This house was very plain and had no magic in it. Daddy drove a truck, but we are not sure what his job was. We walked to worship at Meridian Baptist Church which was near the Chilhowee Cemetery in sight of our home. We remember Daddy carrying Willa Jean and Mother carrying Robert on the way home from church. We called this house our Mad Dog House because one day while Daddy was at work, a rather large dog had a fit

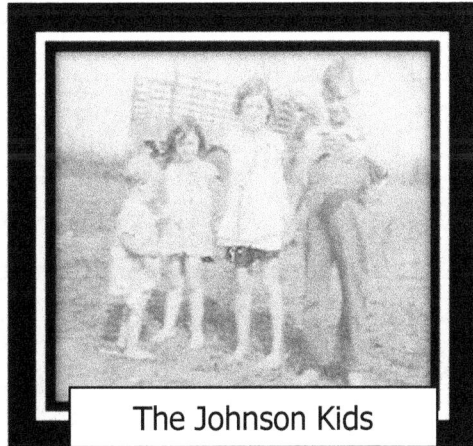

The Johnson Kids

and came into this house. We all climbed up on the table (including Mother). We had our own dog tied to a clothesline, and this dog bit our dog, and so our dog had to be killed. We can't remember what happened to the mad dog. There was nothing neither magic nor beautiful about this place, and even Mother's cardboard piano could not make beautiful music here. We moved from this very plain, white, ugly house as soon as possible. At least the family was all still intact, and all still loved each other.

It was at this time that the Johnson family (the sisters) sold the old home place in Seymour to Aunt Ida and Uncle Clif. This was the beginning of the end of the Johnson dynasty in Seymour, Tennessee. The old maid Johnson sisters moved into a pleasant split level home on Martin Mill Pike in Knoxville. It was in a quiet,

The Mad Dog House

secluded neighborhood which suited their lifestyle. While we all missed the farm with its spacious lawn, rolling hills, and orchard, the Martin Mill Pike home was more convenient for the girls and also for Aunt Pearl who had just recently become a widow when Uncle Mutt died of cancer. He was one of the first in our family to die of cancer, and we were told a plow handle hit him in the side, causing a knot to come up which in turn grew into a large knot eventually killing him. Aunt Pearl moved in with the girls. At that time, it was easy for Mother to persuade our Daddy to visit our Alabama kinsfolk, so all our earthly belongings were stored with relatives and we packed up for an adventurous trip down South.

Chapter 8: First Trip to Alabama

Our first visit to Alabama came in 1934 when our parents decided it was time to leave the "mad dog house" and to look for greener pastures. This was our first official meeting with our Alabama kinsfolk, even though Mother had kept in close contact with her mother with letters throughout the years. We were all so excited about getting to meet our new cousins and grandparents. Daddy was assured by Uncle Bill Berry that work would be available at TVA in Florence. Since Uncle Bill was employed as captain on a riverboat, Daddy felt comfortable about pulling up stakes and returning to the country where he had found the love of his life. His Johnson family was opposed to this move, but so many tragic events had happened in recent years that Daddy was anxious to get away. His dad had died tragically in 1931 of a massive stroke in the field while he was farming. His death was followed by the death of our grandmother in 1934 who died with tuberculosis. These losses of both his parents, his jobs, and his home were enough to make him feel a jinx, and he was ready for a change of scenery. We, all six of us, boarded a train in the center of Knoxville and made the long trip to Sheffield, Alabama. Lucille and Willa Jean got train sick from riding backwards and from the loud, clacking noises of the train wheels. We can still recall the conductor calling out "Sweeeeet...Water...Sweeeeeet...Water" and we were so...sick!!! The only nice thing about the train ride was the fascinating water cooler with the individual cone

shaped cups. We can't remember how many trips we made
to get a drink and how we pestered Mother about what
happened to the waste water in the bathroom. Willa Jean
tried to look down the toilet seat, but she was afraid she
would fall through. Sister had to pull her back as usual.
After departing from the train, we hailed a taxi to four-mile
branch and the home of Mamahatha and Poptoe. We had a
terrific scare when we crossed Wilson Dam. It was our
first time to see a dam, and the walls seemed to literally
moved in on us, and we could feel the water rushing in.
The family were all so happy to see us, and we had never
seen so many people in such a small place in all our lives.
It was not quite daylight when we arrived, but little people
were awake everywhere. Aunt B had six children—
Virginia (GG), Junior, Louise, Bobby, Helen B., and Billy
G. It seemed like twelve at the time, who all lived with
Mamahatha and Poptoe, but everything was so cozy. (At
this time we children realized we no longer called them
Mamo and Paptoe!) The coffee was brewing, hot biscuits
were in the oven, and everyone was talking at once. The
radio, Mamahatha's proudest possession, was blaring above
all the noise, but no one dared touch it. Roy Acuff was
mourning "Great Speckled Bird", and we four children just
gaped. Daddy just laughed, and Mother cried for joy to be
home again.

This joyous reunion was short-lived, however.
Daddy soon found out that the promise of a good job in
Alabama was just as illusive as those had been in
Tennessee. The depression had not been a respecter of
states. All people were suffering. Poptoe and Mamahatha
were taking care of Aunt B's children (she had divorced

Uncle Van), and she had a job at Flagg Knitting Mill in East Florence. She was a good worker and always made production. Her older children hired out to pick cotton. Daddy saw that children were treated a little differently in Alabama, especially around the dinner table and at night time. When dinner was served, the children were told to go outside and wait until the adults had finished eating. Daddy looked astonished! Not his children! At least not without their dad! So he went out with us. This was the first mark against him as a son-in-law. If anything was left, after the children did the

Aunt Beatrice White's children: Virginia, Van Junior, Louise, Bobby Front: Helen B., Billy G

dishes, they could eat it. After this disaster, came bedtime. Children were all told to sleep on the floor. Once again, Oh, no!!! We're sure Mother was humiliated at Daddy's response, but you can guess what it was. By this time, everyone knew what to expect. Dock's kids didn't sleep on the floor!!! Well, it actually didn't

Aunt Elise Berry's children: Betty Jo, Billy Reed, and Dorothy Jean

matter much anyway since the job didn't pan out. Uncle Bill, Aunt Elise's husband was working with TVA. When he saw that there was no job for Daddy at the Knitting Mill, he promised to try with TVA, but Daddy couldn't afford to stay with Poptoe indefinitely so we were soon back on the road again.

Chapter 9: Fifth Avenue (January 1935)

Next to the Mad Dog House, the Fifth Avenue house or apartment in Knoxville holds the ugliest memories. While the apartment itself was nice—it was upstairs, but all on one floor—it seemed cold and uninviting and never seemed like home to us. One of us seemed to be sick all the time. This was the place where we first experienced our taste of calomel. If you have never had that deceiving medicine, don't try it! It looks like tempting pink candy drops, and if you were a child during the thirties, any pink candy drop would have been inviting--but, oh the results! What a "working-out"! Mother said all the moving had made us "wormy", and this was the best remedy she could think of. Since there was no money for Doctors, she was definitely our "medicine woman" of the household. We still remember how her little finger looked as it stirred up the "black draught" with just a little water in a teaspoon. She'd say, "Now, down it all in one swallow—don't spit it back up—or you'll get twice that much more next time!" And so we would—for we invariably spit it back up! Have you ever tasted black draught? If not, then you have never experienced the ultimate sinner's food. We used to pretend it belonged to Satan and his witches. They brewed it at midnight, and somehow Mother got it directly from them. We never questioned how she got it. It always made us sicker than we were before we tasted it, but Mother insisted it gave us a good "cleaning out".

While Mother attended to our medical needs, Daddy tried to help when he could with the spiritual and educational needs. He always seemed larger than life to us, but he was actually only average in height and was always under weight, a little gangly. We don't remember ever having seen him sitting still very long at a time. He never liked to "dress up". That was just the opposite of Mother, who always loved to dress us all in our "Sunday best." There were two instances that we both can recall when Daddy took us four kids on outings alone—once to church and once to a movie. Both times were very unusual experiences for us. Not that we didn't go to church. We did with Mother. Daddy seldom attended, but we belonged to the Southern Missionary Baptist Church, in whatever community we happened to reside, always around the vicinity of Knoxville, but always close enough to walk. We never had a car. Lucille remembers riding in a car, but Willa Jean can't. She remembers trucks, but not going to church in them. Daddy came home from work one Friday afternoon and told us a new "sect" of people had come to town and were holding a week-end of meetings in a tent not far from where we lived. He told us that if we would be good, he would take us there for one of the nights, but we must not laugh or disturb their worship in any way. They were called "Campbellites", and he thought they might be rolling on the grass and speaking in tongues. We were to be very respectful because that was what they believed in. Mother wouldn't go because they didn't believe in having a piano. She thought they were "hardshelled" Baptists. We did not know what that meant, but our imaginations were working overtime by now, and we couldn't wait to see these people with hard shells and with many tongues. To our deep disappointment, none of these things proved to be true. Daddy was probably a little disappointed, too. The singing was pretty even without a piano, and Willa Jean went to sleep during the long sermon. Daddy had to carry her home. She loved for him to carry her for he smelled a little like the shaving soap he kept in a mug mixed with dust he picked up on the railroad tracks and the scent of "Redman" tobacco which he always kept in his shirt pocket. We always felt so safe in Daddy's arms. We were so unaware of what was going on in the world in the early 1930's. Buddy and Sister might have been more aware of our material poverty and of the precarious situation our country was in at that time, but Willa Jean and Robert only knew that the Johnson's were together and happy. What wonderful parents we had!

One other special outing we recall going to with Daddy was to a western picture show or at least we thought that was what it was going to be. Tom Mix, we think it was. We recall so vividly the horses running down the screen. We felt like screaming inside. We just knew those horses were going to hit us before they sidled off to the left or to the right. What was so nice about the movies back then was that the good guys always wore white hats and the bad guys always wore black hats, had beards, and smoked cigars, so you knew what was coming. The heroine usually had Shirley Temple curls and always screamed right at the right time and always fainted in the good guy's arms. The day Daddy took us to the movie there was an intermission which included an interlude of dancing girls doing the cancan routine showing their petticoats and underwear.

Daddy marched us right back up the aisle, and we didn't see the end of the movie. That seemed to be the extent of Daddy's roll in our spiritual and cultural needs.

While we were at Fifth Avenue, we attended Fifth Avenue Baptist Church. It was there that Buddy and Lucille both accepted Christ and were baptized. We remember being involved in church activities, Sunday school, and Bible training. Our stay on Fifth Avenue was rather short, but we did attend school in the city for a while. None of us children liked being transferred to so many different schools, but Mother would always say, "But see how smart it has made you!" Mother and Daddy both tried to make the most of an almost impossible situation here at Fifth Avenue. Our landlady was obnoxious, our classmates were rude, our money was extremely scarce, and our food supply was becoming very low.

So once again, Daddy gave in to the tempting call from Alabama, and the Johnson family packed their bags and headed for greener pastures. This time, however, we stayed in a calmer environment. Aunt E and Uncle Bill opened up their home to us. They had three children, and they had more room for a family of six. There was no work, however, for Daddy. Uncle Bill was crushed, but at this time so many jobs were political in nature, and if you had no pull, especially if you were a Republican in a Democratic environment, you were out in the cold. And so it was with Daddy. It seems ironic that at this time Lucille remembers attending school at Brandon in East Florence. Could, by any chance, her future husband Ralph Wilson have been anywhere on the school campus at that time?

And, if so, how could he not have noticed that young lady with the long brown curls?

We spent Christmas of 1935 in Alabama, but Daddy's pride would not allow him to remain in Uncle Bill's home any longer; so once again we repacked our bags. Our Alabama kinfolk cried and begged us to stay, but Daddy kept thinking that Knoxville was the best place to be during the depression; so back to the train depot we went.

Chapter 10: House by the Pond

This time we moved nearer to Knoxville in a house which was across the road from a pond. It will always be "the house by the pond" to us. We loved living there also. We went to Anderson School. (A poem written by Lucille while she was in school then is shown in the appendix.) We got our first real piano while living there. Daddy walked to the bus line and rode the bus to work. We were near the school and walked to and from. We were also near a very nice Presbyterian church, and we attended church there most of the time. Mother believed in attending the nearest church if possible. Her thought was that we could serve better. Lucille still has book-ends she made in Vacation Bible School at that church. Willa Jean has a cork whatnot Buddy made at that same VBS. We had several unusual events to happen in our lives while living at this place.

Mother always kept in touch with her family back home, regardless of the miles of separation, so she was devastated when she got the news back in October of 1938 that Poptoe had had his arm severed off in a car accident. According to Mamahatha he was riding in a car with his right arm out the right door window, and a truck side-swiped the car. Papa was hospitalized, and the entire family was in a state of shock. He had lost quite a bit of blood and was also in quite a bit of pain. Excerpts from Mamahatha's letter are included in the appendix of this book. She gives a vivid account of the accident and the funeral for the arm, which takes place, incidentally, at Jones Hill Cemetery, where both Mamahatha and Poptoe will later be buried. This letter must have reminded our mother once again of her Indian heritage and just how close our families are to nature. It seems that Poptoe's arm was wrapped carefully in strips of sheets and placed in a box. His hand was placed in a quart fruit jar, along with information concerning the contents of the burial, and was placed at the head of the grave. The children took care of the funeral proceedings while Mamahatha stayed with Poptoe at the hospital. A few days later, according to one of our cousins, the arm began itching and had to be dug up and reburied to make it more comfortable. This time, it rested comfortably, and as far as we can tell, it is still resting in Jones Hill by the side of Mamahatha. Our own dear Mother is also buried there now. This cemetery is a quiet and peaceful place in the midst of a lovely neighborhood called "Evergreen Estates".

At the time of the "funeral of the arm", however, it was an old abandoned cemetery, grown up with weeds and surrounded by a cow pasture. It has graves dating back to the early eighteen hundreds, but it had not been a well kept spot. A few years ago, however, Jan Roblin, of Florence, became quite interested in the cemetery and thanks to her hard work, it has now been recognized as a cemetery of note in Lauderdale County.

And now back to Mother and the bad news she had received. Mamahatha knew that Mother would not be able to make the trip back to Alabama, but she also knew how much Mother missed her family back home. So she corresponded with her on a regular basis. Just after the letter "edged in black", she follows with a letter telling about their getting electricity in "six rooms"—one light in each room! As well as a light on both porches! She only wished Jeannie could see this as well as see all the pretty flowers they had planted. Billy G had started to kindergarten and GeeGee had a new "permanent!" What great news! No wonder Mother laughed through her tears—wiped her eyes and felt good all over again. If only things could keep going well for the Johnson family.

Regardless of how busy we seemed to be at the "Pond", Robert and Willa Jean always found time for a few major escapades. One in particular has been told and re-told with embellishments here and there according to Willa Jean. They had been saving up their pennies for an Easter card for Mother. Finally, after selling a box of Rose-bud salve, they had 10 cents! So away to town they went! There were many ways to go to Knoxville, so they did not pay particular attention. After all, they were 6 and 8 years old, respectively. They should know their way around! But it got dark quite early in Knoxville in April, and their home was about three or four miles outside of Knoxville. They had no trouble finding Gay Street with its department stores, and they selected a beautiful Easter card. On the way back, after passing the old church building and a few more familiar landmarks, which are still there, incidentally, they crossed a bridge they <u>thought</u> was the one they had come over earlier, but it wasn't. They ended up under the bridge on a dark, gloomy street. Robert started kidding Willa Jean by saying he was going to jump in the river! They played along the river bank until almost dark and then decided to ask at a home across the street just where they were. When the lady of the house realized they were lost, she called the police. By this time, a terrified Dock Johnson was in the police station reporting 2 missing children. Oh well, all's well that ends well! At least, almost! Mother's card was still intact! When they got home, Daddy had them to sit down in a chair. He took off his belt, and Willa Jean had never been so terrified! He hit the legs of the chair and made her promise never to run away from home again! But honestly, she was not running away—she was only exploring! The way she usually did! No wonder Buddy and Sister sat with smiles on their faces. They were older and knew better. Robert could plead youthful offender so Willa Jean bore the blame (again)!

In the joshing department Buddy did not get off scot free either, however! We really had fun kidding him about his first girl friend - a skinny young lady who was truly smitten by him. She could play a guitar and sing "In the Pines." Robert, Sister, and Willa Jean spent hours harmonizing that song so when she did sing it to Buddy, he blushed a deep red.

One of the most exciting events that happened while we were living at the Pond was the trip to Knoxville by President Franklin Roosevelt. He rode in a motorcade past our school, and we were allowed to line the highway to wave at him. He had on a tall black hat, and he waved to all the children. Sister and Buddy were very embarrassed at Willa Jean. Remember, we were Republicans, and he was a Democrat, so Willa Jean turned her back and wouldn't look at him. Oh, how she regretted not getting a peep, at least!

While we only lived by the Pond for about two years, these years were filled with memories...mainly dominated by Mother. First, there was the episode of Mother's saving the life of our pet duck. The duck had sat on her eggs for so long that her body had become infected. Mother sewed her up, literally! Mother's bravery was something to behold. She was as brave and courageous as one could be and yet as gentle and kind as one could wish a mother to be. This same mother, who cared so carefully for the duck and held the little ducklings in her hands, warned a stray cat to stay away from her chicks! When the cat refused, Mother took an ax (this is still hard to record) and cut off its head! Sister and Willa Jean went screaming into the house and hid their heads. Mother told them they had to be strong and to protect what was theirs! She also sewed up the neck of their dog when he was bitten by another dog in a fight. We don't think Mother was afraid of anything, and sometimes her Cherokee Indian ancestry came out in full force. There was one episode at the Pond in which both Mother and Daddy showed compassion, but only up to a point. During these post-depression years, there were many homeless people. One woman came by our house by the pond one night wanting something to eat. We children were upstairs, pretending to be asleep. Daddy was a little leery about letting her inside, but Mother allowed her to come to the back door. She made her some gravy and biscuit and coffee. Daddy told her she could sleep in the old out-house back of our house, but to be gone by the time the children got up the next morning. She was. Our parents never mentioned her to us, and we never said we were awake.

Our mother was courageous, brave, compassionate, and caring. She was always watchful for the welfare of her children. During the 1930's the winters were unusually cold. Mother made provisions for us by heating irons on the fireplace and wrapping them with wool cloths and putting them in our beds at night. But during the day, she allowed us to skate on the pond which was covered with a thick layer of ice. She was always careful to see that we had layers of clothes on, caps on our heads, and gloves on our hands. It was here that Buddy got his big red sled from Santa, and we had so much fun sliding over the hill to the edge of the pond.

We spent many hours "sitting" in an old apple tree— reading and eating green apples—but that didn't hurt us. We all loved books, paper dolls and games. Mother would buy material and make our dresses just like Shirley Temple's. She would curl Willa Jean's hair on silk stockings, but it still stuck out on the ends. Sometimes she curled Lucille's hair also even though it was naturally curly.

These years in the house by the pond were busy for us; we were in school and also sang on the radio station KNOX at the movie theater on Saturdays. The program was called "Stars of Tomorrow". We were billed as "The Johnson Quartet". Mother played the piano and we sang. This was unusual because it was the whole family—two girls, two boys, and a mother. Willa Jean and Lucille were also in many other programs, giving recitations ("Readings" as they were called). Mother was a super teacher—leading us in all our activities.

We always lived close enough to our Johnson family to visit often. We remember Aunt Grace and Aunt Ruth combing and curling our hair. They were so proud of us and loved all of us so much. They also encouraged us to sing and recite. Daddy was very protective and would not let us spend any time away from him and Mother, but we really did not want to.

Christmas was always important to our family because it was also Robert's birthday, Santa Claus time, and special church activities. Mother saved some of our letters to Santa.

We really have many memories of our life while living "by the pond." The house was actually across the road from the pond. We were about a half-mile from a small grocery store and not far from Anderson School in Seymour, Tennessee.

While we children were blissfully happy at home and at school, things were not going so well financially for Daddy and Mother. Mother had tried to help Daddy by working temporarily at a clothing factory, but she was never able to get to work on time mainly because she did not believe in clocks and also because she could not bring herself to leave her children and her piano.

The Dock Johnson Family 1936

Chapter 11: Candora Avenue 1937-1939

They were the best of times...they were the worst of times..." Charles Dickens would agree with us, we think, about our last abode in Knoxville. Daddy was finally gainfully employed (at least employed) at Chavannes Lumber Company, bringing in a regular salary, averaging about ten to twelve dollars per week, so we thought we were finally on the road to prosperity. But wait--debtors can't be choosers! There are always vultures waiting in the wings—ready to take what they can at any cost—among them were insurance companies, federal old age payroll taxes, and even a garnishment by Dr. L. O. Blalock, for an unknown amount, so we didn't have much to celebrate with, but we were happy anyway. (See Appendix)

There were many good reasons for our moving to Candora. First of all, it was closer to Daddy's work, and since he had found a second job at Vestal Marble Works, he could walk to work, which saved us quite a bit. Secondly, the little house was quite charming with a split level, made just for Mother to plant beautiful flowers all around. Daddy also was allowed to bring scrap marble home from work so he made a marble walkway which Mother lined with zinnias, old-maids, and lark spurs. Both Mother and Daddy were very proud of this home, the first with electricity—but still with no running water. We still lived "on the other side of the tracks" literally—but we were too happy to mind it.

Everyday after working all day, Daddy carried water from a neighbor's house to water his flowers. We also had to carry water to wash. We all worked hard to make our home a happy, successful home. Daddy bought Buddy and Sister bicycles so they could carry the Knoxville Journal, our local newspaper. We all helped to carry the papers on two long paper routes which covered quite a large territory up on Candora Hill. Later, Daddy took on a third job as collector for the Knoxville Journal.

During all our many moves, our parents made sure we were in school and that we were never behind in our school work. Despite the fact that we changed schools frequently during the year, we always seemed to end up near the top of the class academically. At the time we moved to Candora, Buddy (13) and Sister (11), had been promoted to Young High School in 9th and 10th grades. Willa Jean was 9 in the 6th grade and Robert was 7 in the 4th grade at Vestal School. We all walked to school. Robert and Willa Jean walked the railroad tracks to Vestal (how dangerous!) as far as the overpass and then on to school. Aunt Grace was Robert's teacher, and the only time Willa Jean got mad at Aunt Grace was when she spanked Robert on his hand for not paying attention in class. We all loved school (except Robert).This was the first time we had had an opportunity to be involved socially with other young people our age. Sister and Buddy were very happy in the band. All of us took piano lessons from mother (Buddy and Robert both reluctantly). Willa Jean and Lucille learned a number of Daddy's favorite religious songs, including, "Shall We Gather at the River" and "Sowing in the Morning", but the song Lucille most wanted to learn was

"We've a Story to Tell to the Nations." She wanted to be able to play this for the G.A.'s girls' mission group in the Baptist church, and this she accomplished. This song was written in the key of F, and after these many years, this song has now been written in the key of A flat.

Attending Young High School in Knoxville was a wonderful experience for Sister and Buddy. They had their first music lessons from someone other than Mother or the Johnson aunts. Mr. Still was the band instructor and choral director. Lucille really enjoyed both the band and the singing. Her love for classical music began during those years. Lucille played the coronet or trumpet, Buddy played the clarinet. In chorus, Lucille sang first or second soprano. Music was a credited course in Tennessee. Buddy had a very helpful two years in "Home Ec for Boys" and woodwork. He learned how to cook and really enjoyed making things in woodwork. Lucille had always planned to be a home economics teacher some day. That had always been her plan and dream. She changed her mind later and decided that music was really her love. Her favorite compositions were Liebestraum's "Dream of Love" and "Come Oh Spring". Buddy and Willa Jean later became our "teachers" continuing our family tradition of teachers. You'll hear more about these later. It was at Young High School that Sister met Gordon Sams, on whom she had her first big crush! (He didn't know it!) Later, his sister married a Crittenton from Florence, Alabama, and Sister went to church with the family later in life.

Church was a big part of life at this time. We were all actively involved. Mother and Sister both played the piano. Mother was involved in WMU (Women's

Missionary Union) at Emanuel Baptist Church. It was here that Willa Jean and Robert were baptized.

Family was still very important to us, and the Davis family (Aunt Daisy's family) became great friends to us since they lived directly across the street from the church. Uncle Stuart was a very stern person, and expected perfection from his children. There were six children in that family; one daughter, Elizabeth, and five sons Buddy, Murel, Joe, Bill, and Jack. We don't remember Uncle Ern, Daddy's oldest brother, but we do remember Ray, EllaRee's older brother. He was tall, solemn, and very dignified. Bill and our Buddy spent many happy hours together. Bill and his wife, Maxine, still live in Knoxville. At this time, Ella Ree Johnson, Uncle Ern's daughter, went to the Methodist Church where she played the piano, also, but she would meet Sister after church. Ella Ree was older and was dating some at this time. We loved to go to her home since Aunt Maude was a great cook. Our Rogers' cousins were Methodists and lived in Seymour County. When we could, we visited with them and had a great time on the farm. We helped make cottage cheese. This was at Aunt Ina's house, and we all got to sleep upstairs on pallets on the floor. There were four girls in this family—Margaret, Katherine, Dorothy and Hughella. This was the only family that Daddy allowed us to spend the night with. All the cousins in Aunt Ina's family were around our age. Daddy and Uncle Hugh were also great friends and enjoyed spending time together. Aunt Ina and Mother loved to talk about their children. Many people thought Mother and Aunt Ina looked very much alike.

One little cousin that Willa Jean was allowed to play with quite frequently was Mary Evelyn Ford—who was her same age. Aunt Ida Ford was overly protective of Mary Evelyn since she was an only child. Mary Evelyn never seemed to fit in with all the other rambunctious cousins. Oh, how Aunt Ida wanted her to be like Willa Jean, who would have liked to have spent more time with her. Uncle Cliff and Aunt Ida made every effort to make life wonderful for their only child.

One of the most beautiful and talented cousins in our Johnson's family was Lady Ruth Burch, daughter of H. A. and Kathryn Burch. She was also an only child. However, she was extremely healthy, beautiful, and talented. She was about two years younger than Robert and seemed to fit right in with the Johnson clan when she visited in Tennessee, but she was living at this time in Tupelo, Mississippi, where her Daddy was Superintendent of Education and her mother was a teacher.

It was also during a visit to the Burch's in Mississippi that the youngest Johnson, Mildred, met her husband, Hershael Wheeler, who was Sheriff of Iuka, Mississippi; they later had two children, Joe and Joan, who were our youngest cousins who came much later in life. Joan was also extremely talented in music and became a talented organist, but this is getting ahead in our storehouse of memories.

In spite of all the time we spent with our cousins, our church, and our schools, we still made time to visit the library and read, read, read. Our entire family (except Daddy) read every available minute. Before we had electricity, we read by lamplight. We can't remember when

Mother didn't read us the paper and a bedtime story. She also took the time to sing us songs before bedtime. We never grew too old for that. Our love for music and recitation did not stop at home. We were also quite active in programs in church as well as programs on the radio. We belonged to a little club at KNOX called "Stars of Tomorrow" where we performed as the Johnson Quartet. We enjoyed the singing as well as the rewards—chocolate cakes for birthdays and free Saturday morning matinees. Some of the favorite songs we sang at KNOX were "Wait for the Wagon," "Cape Town Races," for traditional singing and for religious songs such old favorites as "Put My Little Shoes Away" and "I Need the Prayers of Those I Love." Perhaps the reason we were successful in this endeavor was that it was a little unusual to have four children under the ages of 14 who could harmonize in all four parts. What was not known was how many hours Mother spent singing with us and coaxing Robert to sing along with the rest of us and threatening to pinch us all if Robert didn't sing up! And so, he did—with his mischievous ways. Mother sang each part with us separately. Sister sang second soprano (men's tenor); Buddy sang bass; Willa Jean, alto; and Robert, the lead. Mother was always our pianist, our inspiration, and a great performer! (See appendix)

Our performing was not only limited to singing, but it also was in readings and recitations, which were so popular during the 1920's and 1930's. Some of the most requested recitations performed by Sister were "Mother's Angel Child Dines Out," a four page reading about Mother and her mischievous child, and "Vacation Time" which was always popular. Willa Jean recited "Hello Santa Claus" a soliloquy about a little girl who thinks Santa sounds "just like her daddy" and "Encouragement", a humorous soliloquy about a young black girl and her sweetheart, Ike Johnson. We also tried our hands at writing poetry. At a very early age, Sister composed a poem called "Thanksgiving," which was in the Anderson School News in 1936. (See copy in appendix.) There were also plays at school in which the Johnson kids were involved. Sister was Penrod's sweetheart in some comedy called "Penrod and Sam." We loved to go to and to participate in community affairs.

Not all community affairs were pleasant, however. We wanted to be fair to the entire family so we went with Daddy to the community boxing matches which Mother and the girls detested. Boxing was a popular sport during the 30's. Our old family dog, Spot #2, who has a history all of his own, loved to follow us to these boxing matches, but we didn't dare take him because he would let out such a howl. We first met Spot when Daddy brought him home while we were living at the house by the pond. He quickly made himself a member of our family and fit right in as a seventh member.

In spite of all our extra curricular activities, Daddy was still coping with three jobs—Chavannes Lumber Company, during the day, Vestal Marble works part-time in the afternoons, and collecting for the Knoxville Journal— our days were long. Knoxville Journal was a morning paper so we all had to rise before daybreak. Mother cooked breakfast early so we could deliver papers and get back home in time to get ready for school. Daddy and Mother never complained so we accepted this as part of our teamwork. Robert and Willa Jean rolled papers and delivered the ones close by while Buddy and Sister rode their bikes up Candora Hill where there were lots of barking dogs and delivered the paper to people like Lowell Blanchard, manager of the radio station KNOX at that time. Mr. Blanchard owned one of the dogs that terrified Sister. After all the children had returned from paper routes and had left for school and Daddy had left for work, Mother had the day for church activities, sewing, playing the piano, writing music, and working on programs for the quartet. Our dinner was usually about 5 p.m., when Daddy would get in from his collection job for Knoxville Journal.

On October 30, 1939, Mother began supper at the usual time. We were all at home. Spot was asleep under the floor. Mother had potato soup with cornbread, and she was keeping it warm on the back of the stove. Daddy was late. It became dark—but still we waited. Then we heard a brisk knock at the door. We were all apprehensive—all in the kitchen. Two policemen came in. They told Mother there had been an accident and that Daddy had been injured and was in critical condition at Baptist Memorial Hospital. They offered to take her to the hospital. We think Buddy went with her, and they took Sister, Willa Jean, and Robert to Aunt Grace's on Martin Mill Pike. In the meantime, Spot had not stopped his howling which he had started before the police arrived.

According to the police, Daddy was crossing the street at East Church Avenue just after dark when he was struck by a car driven by a veteran cook at the University of Tennessee. Daddy had started to the other side of the street, and he didn't see the car. The car was coming too fast, and he started back to return to the curb, but when he was trying to dodge the car, he was struck down. At the time he had a pencil and a notebook in his hand. The driver said the accident was unavoidable because of the dim street lights. When Mother arrived at the hospital, she was at first not allowed to see Daddy. Then later the Doctors came out and told her that the injuries were so severe they recommended that surgery not be performed. Mother refused to go along with this recommendation. Daddy had severe leg and shoulder injuries, a deep gash on his jawbone and his chin, but he never lost consciousness. His worst injuries took place when he was knocked up into the air and fell back on the car ornament on the radiator. After all these injuries, we think the actual cause of his death may have been from his developing pneumonia.

Daddy was injured on October 30, 1939, two days after Willa Jean's birthday, and he died November 9, 1939, two days after Sister's birthday. Daddy's body lay in state at the home of the Aunts on Martin Mill Pike. We remembered how the Aunts had to plead with us children to leave our home on Candora to spend the night with them. Spot howled continuously throughout these days. We had to tie him at home, so we didn't want to leave. Neither did we want to see our Daddy's body in an open casket in Aunt Grace's living room! There were so many people and so many beautiful flowers. Mother looked lost, but her Alabama family was there to comfort her. She looked so pretty, but she was all in black. The funeral took place on November 11, 1939, at Emanuel Baptist Church. As was expected, Mother chose the music. The same songs were also used at Mother's funeral sixteen years later. Twenty-nine years after Mother's death, Sister's husband, Ralph

Wilson died. These same songs were used at his funeral. The songs included "Sunrise Tomorrow," "Twilight is Falling," "It Is Well With My Soul." These songs have stayed close to our hearts these many years, and we will probably request them to be sung at our own funerals. Berry Funeral Home was in charge of the arrangements and transported Daddy's body for the last time to Seymour, Tennessee, back to his roots in the foothills of the Great Smoky Mountains. There he was buried next to his mother and father in Chilhowee Cemetery, just over the hill from the old home place, the house on the hill, and the vacant lot where the Pitner House used to be. (See Appendix)

Our lives were totally crushed. Physically, only Daddy died, but emotionally, an entire family died with him. We didn't know where to turn, literally. Mother's family came rushing to the rescue with hats, gloves, veils, and love. They couldn't understand our reluctance to leave Knoxville.

Mother & children at Daddy's grave.

On the other hand, our heart-broken Johnson Aunts couldn't understand why we would even think about leaving. They said they were not only losing a brother—they were

Chilhowee Cemetery.

losing their children, also. Mother was in a daze. She had never worked, had never had to worry about making the final decisions. She was suddenly faced with the responsibility of taking care of four teen-agers. She had no insurance, no job, no car—if she had had a car, she couldn't drive. Aunt Beatrice promised her a job at the knitting mill in Sweetwater, Florence, Alabama. Mother had heard of those promises before, but this time she had to believe. She had no recourse. So once again, it was pack up, load up, and off to Alabama except this time it was for a family of five, and it was final. There would be no turning back.

Chapter 12: Alabama 1939-40

Alabama was ugly, cold, miserable, and the entire Dock Johnson family hated it. But it was not Alabama's fault. Different Johnson families had offered to take different Johnson children to raise as their own: Aunt Kate wanted Robert for a big brother for Lady Ruth; Aunt Ida wanted Willa Jean for a sister to Mary Evelyn, the old maid aunts wanted Sister and Buddy. Mother and children would not even discuss the separation. Mamahatha and Poptoe opened up their home to us. It was already filled with Aunt B and her six children. We really had fun here but our hearts were still grieving and we did not have a proper place to grieve. About a month after we arrived in Alabama, Daddy's company insurance money that Mother was not aware was due came through, and she bought a house at 319 Middle Road, Florence. After buying a 1939 Pontiac, she gave the remainder of her money to Uncle Walter for material for a new home for him and Aunt Barbara. Mother hired a driver and rented a truck for Buddy (who was only 15) to go to Knoxville to pack up all our earthly belongings and bring them down to Alabama. Poor Buddy had to make the decisions on what was important to bring back and what had to be discarded. He was already grown up way beyond his age and would suffer much more mentally and physically for years as a result of these tragic few months that completely devastated his family. He become head of the house—making all the important decisions as Mother grew more and more despondent over blows life had dealt her. We are sure at this time she turned to her mother many times for solace and even for future outlook from "cards" and "grounds". Mamahatha was always there for her, but she always had a house filled with others to care for also, and Mother was aware of the gap between her and Poptoe even at this time in her life. When Buddy pulled up at 319 Middle Road on arrival from Knoxville with all our

House on Middle Rd.

belongings, out jumped "Old Spot" and we had a Johnson reunion—right where the Lauderdale County Board of Education now stands. One of the worst experiences we had in coping with our new life was getting adjusted to the Alabama school system. (Little did we dream that we would become so involved in the educational field in Alabama.) On our first day of school, Willa Jean was told by her 8th grade teacher, Mrs. Hackworth (oh, how apropos her name), to have all her books by the next day and bring her report card if she expected to be in the 8th grade at her early age. Oh, how she hated that woman! The only bright spots in that room were when she received smiles from Lester Hibbett and his future bride Elaine Williams. Another friendly face was James Coburn. Naturally none of our belongings had arrived from Knoxville yet. Our books were still packed back at home. Report cards had not been available to be picked up. Sister and Buddy found that they had credits taken from them because Alabama did not acknowledge music as a credit. Even though we had never had any problems academically, changing states as well as books was an abrupt change that took some adjusting to. Sister and Buddy were older and had no problem adjusting. They, too, however, had demands such as books to be bought and credits and records to be turned in to the office of the school. Their music was an asset in that it opened doors to them socially and made their teachers more lenient about waiting for their credits. Robert, we suppose, had it easier than the rest. He was enrolled at St. Florian Elementary School and caught the bus right outside our front door. The school was run by the

Tootie Mitchell & Willa Jean at Wildwood Park.

Catholic Church and was administered by Catholic nuns, who were extremely kind and understanding. However, when Willa Jean decided to skip school, Robert was really ready and willing to skip with her—and so skip school, they did! But that's a story within itself.

Robert at St. Florian School.

After about a week of harassment from Mrs. Hackworth, Willa Jean could take no more, but decided on her own to become self-educated. She continued to ride the bus from Middle Road to Coffee

Junior High, but from that parking lot, she very dangerously walked down to the campus of what is now Wesleyan Hall and was at that time a training school for teachers. Here she met Gee Gee White, her cousin who was enrolled there and was Buddy's age, but was in Willa Jean's grade in school, and she would check out books for Willa Jean to take to Wildwood Park to spend a leisurely day reading. Then she would return in the afternoon in time to catch the bus to come home. It's rather ironic that years later Willa Jean would have her own office in Wesleyan Hall when she was a graduate student, acting as instructor of student teachers and as an instructor of "Human Growth and Development." But back in 1939 she was only interested in self survival which was quite precarious at that time. Mr. Hibbett, principal of the school, met Willa Jean as she entered the bus about mid-November and kindly asked her to bring her mom with her to school the next day. Now she knew— reality had set in—the imaginary world in which she had daydreamed that her Daddy was still alive and would come to Alabama for all of them again, Mother would stop crying and we would all be happy again, and most of all that she would never have to see old Hackworth again, was no more. Well, only one of those dreams came true. Mr. Hibbett was so nice. He realized what the family was going through. He knew we didn't have money for books, and he knew Willa Jean was going through a period of severe depression. After looking at her report card that had finally arrived from Knoxville he knew she should be making good grades at Coffee. So he suggested that Mother keep her at home for the entire next semester so that she could go through a period of grieving. Even then, she would be a year younger than her classmates so there would be no stigma in being held back. Mother agreed, so the year 1940 would begin on a brighter note for Willa Jean.

Lucille and Buddy, on the other hand, had their music to help them adjust emotionally through this traumatic part of their young lives. In 1939 Coffee High School band had neither uniforms nor a full-time director. Mr. Schuba, a small, quiet man met with the music students about once a week. Everyone was so surprised that Sister and Buddy were so

Happy days with the Johnson Quartet.

knowledgeable in music. Mary Lucille went to the alto horn, and Buddy continued with his clarinet. Sister sat beside Sam Phillips (who later became famous for his recording studio "Sun Recording" discoverer of Elvis Presley). Sam played the tuba horn. George Hibbett sat on the left, playing the alto horn. Lucille (most people in Alabama dropped the Mary from her name) was in the glee club also.

Everything was so different and strange to Buddy and Lucille at Coffee High. While at Young High in Knoxville they were well known and happy with their student friends and teachers, at Coffee they were almost ignored by all. It is really amusing that 55 years later at the '42 class reunion some of the guys would look at Lucille with a question in their mind and say, "Where were you all that time, I just can't place you in our group?" She would reply, with a laugh, "I was that little girl with long curls and sashes on my dresses." Well, so much for breaking into the city of Florence social circles.

Our acceptance at the local churches was entirely different. Mother was a firm believer in worshipping at the nearest church, if possible. We had been raised in the Baptist faith, but Central Baptist Church in East Florence was at least three miles away, so we visited the Weeden Heights Methodist. Very often we really loved it there and made so many friends that are still friends with us today—Christine Goodman, her brothers and little sister Jean, Doris Holt, Pete and Buck Glover, the Wylie family, and many more.

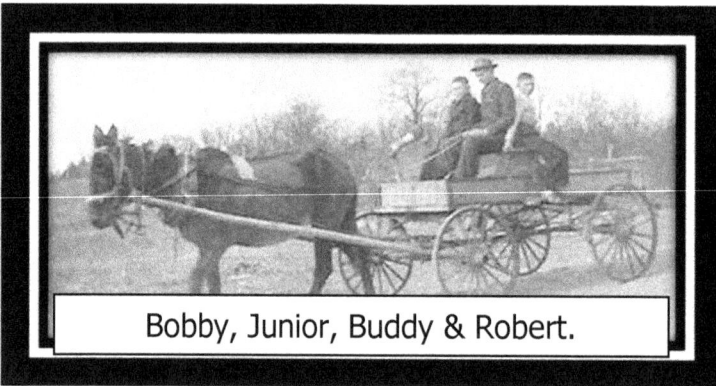

Bobby, Junior, Buddy & Robert.

Even though we were all still so sad about losing our wonderful daddy, having nightmares and bad dreams every night, we slowly adjusted to our new life in our little "country house." Our cousins helped so much here. They came to our house or we went to Mamahatha's daily.

Remember, we were city slickers and knew nothing about a garden or farm animals. Mother thought that buying an old cripple mule "Jack" and a soulful eyed cow would help us be better acquainted with real life that was ahead for us. She gathered up some chickens from some of the family, and we were set to start farm life. We needed some responsibilities to keep us at home and busy while she worked at the knitting mill each day. After all, this was the first property Mother had ever bought on her own, and she was so very proud of her accomplishment. The property included five acres of land facing Middle Road with a 6-room house, an outhouse, and a barn with a high loft. We think it was the barn that gave Mother the idea for the mule, the cow, the chickens, and all the labor she assigned us.

Four Johnson kids at the barn.

And that she truly did! She probably thought the work would take our minds off Daddy's death, but it was not quite successful. First, she brought home a large armful of sweet potato plants and told us to make "mud baths" for them and to plant them the next day. We probably knew as much about it as she did, which was not much. So we deliberated for a while then went into action. The potato plants were buried in the corner of the lot in a deep hole. Mother never asked about them, and we never told. The Johnson kids stuck together (except for Robert). Sometimes he had to be bribed. But that, too, was easy to do.

Mother hated every hour she worked away from home and cried so much. Knitting mill work just wasn't her cup of tea. She was late for work so much, making it harder on her. Other women at the mill were jealous of her because she was still so pretty and she dressed up too much for "production" work. No other work was available for her. It was 1939, and our country was just coming out of a severe depression which was still with our family. Mother's check would average $8 to $10 each week. She never made production.

All of us children learned to cook some, trying to help out, yet we really did not realize the great burden on Mother's shoulders—the responsibility of caring for the home and teenage children in addition to working full time.

Music was her temporary escape from all the many problems in our lives. Many Sundays were spent going to "all day singings". Naturally, the Johnson Quartet was expected to sing, so again, we gathered around Mother and learned new songs. (See index for copies of songs.) It was during this time that Mother met and became very good

Papa and Mamahatha

friends with "Mom and Dad" Spear from Tennessee. The whole Spear Family remained friends with Mother through out her life. We loved to travel with Mother and friends to "all day singings and dinners on the ground" for several reasons: riding on a flatbed truck with our feet hanging off, singing while we were traveling, and eating, eating, eating. We also loved to see the different towns we visited. Some were Haleyville, Phil Campbell, Lawrenceburg, Athens, and other places of "interest." Food was all brought by local people and as singers we were treated as guests. We liked that, too. Mother not only played for us to sing, she also played for different singers to lead the congregation in singing. In a different setting we also went with Mother to what is called the "Fa Sol La or Sacred Harp "singing. We still have some of her books. These singings were much more difficult, but Mother loved these also. In later years, Mother was chosen as pianist for the Lauderdale Gospel Association as well as pianist for Lauderdale Baptist Association (churches from Colbert and Lauderdale Counties). This was a great honor for Mother and brightened her life again.

During these days of quiet desperation, Mother was trying as hard as she could to make life normal for us. If

Lucille & Willa Jean

Spot could ride all the way home from Knoxville to Florence, then jump off the truck in our arms without howling, everything must be going in the right direction. Sister and Buddy had made great friends at school, and we had wonderful cousins to play with. They were all about our ages so we shared in our "farm" work. Virginia was about Buddy's age, next came Junior (Van C.), Louise, Bobby, Helen B., and Billy G. They all lived with Mamahatha. Our younger cousins, Aunt Elise and Uncle Bill's children Dorothy Jean, Billy Reed, and Betty Joe, were always nearby but not old enough to be included in many of our escapades. Uncle Walter's son, Ray, was one of our favorite little cousins, and he was too young to be included. Many years later, Uncle Walter and Aunt Barbara had two daughters Tracy and Tony. How mother would have loved to have known these sweet girls! They were born after mother's death in 1955. Since we all loved to go to Weeden Heights to watch the baseball games, Mother promised us we could all go if we worked out the garden! So, we got in the wagon, hitched up our old crippled Jack (the mule), packed lunch, blankets to sit on, guitars to play, books to read, and went to the field to work for a while. Later, we went home, got dressed, and went to the ball game. Poor Mother never saw the results of the garden, but she did hear the results of the ball game. Some of the outstanding players were Willie Goodwin, the Hunt brothers, James Marshall, and Buck Glover.

Our cousins had told us if we could find enough crickets to kill, we could turn them upside down and it would rain, and we wouldn't have to work! It didn't work!! There were other farm chores as well. Old Bessie had to be staked out and milked, Jack had to be fed and the little old Shetland Pony of Robert's had to survive someway; so we had plenty of work to do. Bessie liked the Johnson grass (no relation) around Middle Road, but she kept getting tangled up in her rope! She also had to be watered and we had to draw the water! She was so thirsty. We never knew a cow could drink so much—mules and ponies too. Jack liked to get out and run away, but he couldn't go far on three legs so Robert and Willa Jean's job was to corner and catch him. We always got the worst jobs! Sister and Buddy were the supervisors, naturally! The little pony liked to come to the back door for food, so we didn't need to keep him tied. Both these animals would come in handy later when Willa Jean and Robert decided to play hooky from school. In the meantime, the four Johnson children attempted to make life easier for their mother by cooking and keeping house. Since Willa Jean was excused from school for the remainder of 39-40 school year, the biggest burden was on her, but all four shared in all the work.

Our first year with our Alabama cousins was 52 weeks full of exciting, fun days, learning so many new things. Our grandparents really had their hands full with 10 of us. We were not accustomed to being bossed around or told so many things we could not do. For example, Poptoe once told Robert to do something trivial, and Robert forgot to do it. The next thing he knew, Poptoe had struck him across the face. We don't know who was the most surprised, Robert, Poptoe, or all the rest of us. Of course, this was the first thing we told Mother when she got home from work. Little did we realize we were adding just one more item on her list of danger signals toward a nervous breakdown. She gathered up her baby boy (who, of course, was spoiled, but was still her youngest) and told him to try to forget what had happened. "After all," she stated, "he is not your real Grandaddy, anyway." We heard, but did not understand the meaning for many years to come. At that time, it only meant that our real grandparents were our Johnson relatives in Knoxville.

Poptoe, as we called him when we were still living in Knoxville, was not unkind to us. We were always a little in awe of him; perhaps because of his one arm and the mystique surrounding the burial of his arm as well as his being able to eat "raw" meat. He used to go to the cellar and cut off a piece of ham, slice an onion, and grab a piece of cornbread for a mid-afternoon snack. Their house was across from what is now the Darby Estate on Lee Highway. Mamahatha spent many hours showing us how to witch for money or water back behind her house. She also knew many methods of planning for a successful day. After breakfast, which always smelled so good (fresh coffee, ham, biscuits), she used the coffee grounds to see what sort of day we would have. If it looked bad, she went for a deck of cards for a better or closer look. If that old Jack of spades showed up, her eyes turned dark, and she re-shuffled the deck. Then things would become quiet around the Mahatha household until she found out for sure just what the day would bring. In the meantime, on radio Roy Acuff would be singing softly in the background. We can still hear him singing the "Great Speckled Bird." If all was well, she wished her eldest daughter goodbye (Mother would already be late for work.), and we would all start on our daily chores.

While we enjoyed being with all our Alabama kinfolk, we still preferred being with "just the five Johnsons." We shared a closeness that is hard to describe to anyone who has not gone through the tragedy we had gone through. Buddy accepted the role as "Head" of the household and Robert turned to him with all his problems and questions. One of the first things he wanted to do was learn to drive a car, but he was only ten years old. Buddy solved that problem by putting a cushion under him and a hat on his head. Robert learned quickly! They even learned to do tricks, going over the hood while one was driving. However, even tricks and fun could not keep our family from seeing the tragedy that was unfolding all around us.

Chapter 13: Early 1940's

The dark clouds of the 30's were beginning to disappear in the nation as well as in the Johnson home. At last, the Great Depression was disappearing just as World War II was looming in the near distance. Already, Great Britain and France were involved, and the United States was on the brink of entering into the war. Business was beginning to boom as a result of this turmoil, so jobs were becoming more available. On the Johnson home front, the sad tones of the 30's were slowly giving way to the more enlightening music of the early

Robert 1940

40's. After leaving Coffee Junior High, Willa Jean had finally settled into St. Florian in 8th grade and seemed to be somewhat content. She and Robert both rode the bus to school. Speaking of trips, the most memorable trip in the early 40's was the one made by Buddy, Sister, Willa Jean and Robert in

Lucille & Buddy 1940-42

the spring. As soon as school was out, Buddy was 16, and Mother consented to our going back to Knoxville alone.

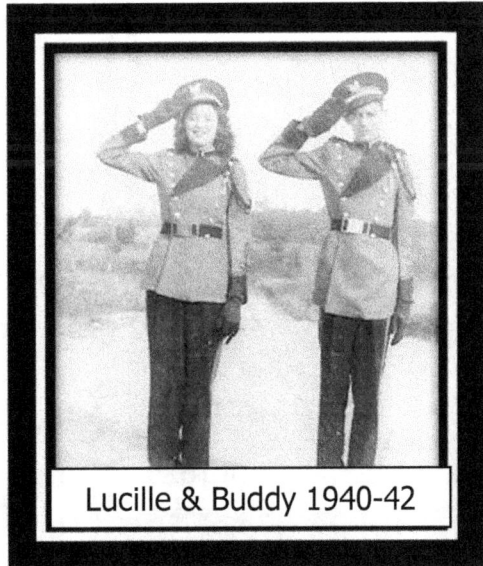

We had no idea how long we would stay or exactly how we would get there. We went through Chattanooga with Buddy driving, and did we all feel important! The aunts were so happy to see us. We were finally able to see Knoxville without looking through tears, but we could not go back to Candora Avenue. We don't remember how much money we took, but we spent it very quickly. We had to send back to Mother for more money to come home on. Sister visited many of her friends. She took advantage of being in Knoxville to visit her church friends. Buddy perhaps visited with friends at the Holstin golf course where he had caddied before Daddy died. He also visited with the Davis family, for he was a good friend as well as a cousin of Bill. We are not sure what Robert did, but he probably followed Buddy, which would have been okay with Buddy. Willa Jean, the loner, spent her time reading the aunts' magazines; Ladies Home Journal, Good Housekeeping, etc.; anything that had a good story to it. She spent one night with Mary Evelyn, who was now living at the old home place in Seymour. We all visited our Rogers cousins who lived on a farm out from Seymour. We stayed with them a few days, and by this time we were ready to head back to Mother and to Alabama. We had our last Christmas together in 1940, and for some reason, everything seemed blurred about that event.

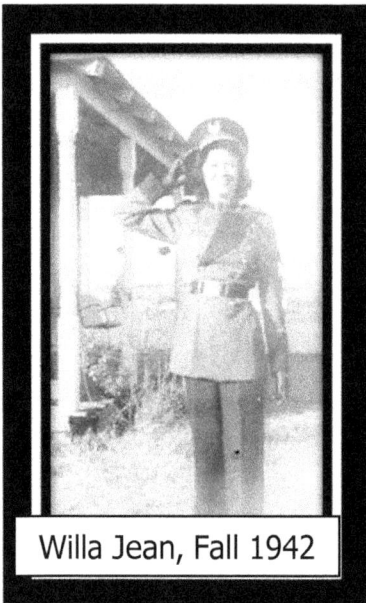

Willa Jean, Fall 1942

The 1940-41 school year was a pivotal one for all the Johnson kids. Robert had Willa Jean in the same school with him, so he couldn't play hooky anymore. At least, unless she did also. Willa Jean was now happy with her new friends and wonderful teacher. We can still see Sister Eugenia flying around the baseball bases with her black skirts flying in the wind! She played hard and taught hard and expected results from her students. She was a wonderful teacher who recognized a lost bewildered young girl when she saw one and took her to her heart. The student body also accepted other students for who they were. Some of the friends we met in St. Florian included Helen Muse, Betty Harrison Hibbett, and Lucille Richey. While we were fascinated with the Catholic religion, Buddy could now drive, so we now attended Central Baptist Church in East Florence where we moved our membership from Knoxville.

It was about this time that we children began to forget that we needed to look out for the needs of our mother. We were beginning to spread our wings. Mother was trying to cope with four teenagers-ages 11, 13, 15, 17-all deeply troubled, looking for happiness, but not knowing where to look. Sister and Buddy were involved in school activities at Coffee High School at this time. Mr. Floyd McClure had been hired as the first band director and our first uniforms of black and gold were on display. Our head majorette was Vera Castleberry, a beautiful brunette, who wore the gold, and Sarah Paulk, an attractive blonde, who wore the black. Sister played French horn, and Buddy played clarinet. This was the first year that a school used what is now Braly Stadium. Sister and Willa Jean were beginning to date—Willa Jean because Sister couldn't go without a chaperone and Sister because she was so cute. About this time, we made a pledge never to date the same boy. Whoever dated the boy first got to keep him. We never had a problem. Most of our dates consisted of a movie or program at school or church, and we had to be home by eight o'clock. Buddy had to know who the boys were. Ironically, he had not screened his own friends at this

Lucille at 16.

Willa Jean at 16.

time. He had started running with a wild group who could see the clouds of war hovering over the country and were trying to get in all the fun and wild life they could before the big war to end all wars began. Buddy joined this group in some wild escapades which landed him in trouble with Mother as well as causing problems with his grades at school. About this time, just as the turmoil was beginning in the Johnson family, Pearl Harbor was attacked on December 7, 1941. Our world was torn apart, literally. By January 1942, Buddy had joined the

Army, Robert had quit school again, and Sister was up to her old tricks! She always had a standing date with her boyfriend of about six months. Since he had enlisted in the Navy, she assumed he was gone, so she accepted a date with another friend (next in line). What a surprise! Saturday night when she looked out the window, she saw both guys in their cars on the way to her house. This is one time she wished that Willa Jean would break her promise and accept one of her rejects. But oh no, Willa Jean refused to cooperate. Mother overheard this intriguing conversation, and she immediately made the decision to ask Buddy, who was home on leave, to meet with both young men (remember he had to know all our friends). He suggested that all three young men find dates for the night—his sister was all tied up. Just imagine a Saturday night and no date!

Most of our get-togethers were with boys and girls— "walking"—and such games as "post office", "spin the bottle," "fruit basket turn over." We never dated alone. Most of the time the cars were filled with teenagers, four in the front, four in the back. Many cars had "rumble seats." No couple ever tried to go out on their own, and no one tried to take advantage of a date. It was all "above board". One of the most popular excursions was the Saturday afternoon matinee at the Princess or the Majestic Theater in Florence where there was an ongoing series called The Iron Claw. The admission was 10 cents, with popcorn for 5 cents. The popular place to sit was in the balcony so popcorn could not be thrown down in your hair.

It was in the Spring of 1942 that Sister met the love of her life—Ralph Wilson, driver of a Hoover Truck.

Mother would not let Sister date him because he had
dropped out of school, but that did not faze Sister. Away
she went with Willa Jean in the back of the truck, and the
romance began. Ralph also knew the way to Sister's heart
was through her siblings; so he let Robert, who was almost
12, drive his <u>big</u> <u>truck</u>—talk about hero worship!

Buddy

Buddy & Lucille

Robert, Mother, Buddy,
Lucille & Willia Jean

Chapter 14: Mary Lucille

My first meeting with Ralph was an example of my life with him (fun and exciting). We met at a Carnival in the Spring of 1942. He was with several friends, and I was with two of my best friends - Billie Mitchell and Helen Goodwin. They both knew the guys with Ralph, and after walking around and playing some of the games, they wanted to take us home. Even though I thought Ralph was extremely cute and had a wonderful personality, I hopped into the back with another guy and pushed Helen into the front seat with Ralph. That did

Ralph & Lucille

not stop him. The following Sunday night, he sat right behind me at Central Baptist Church. At that time, he told the friends with him, "I'm going to marry that girl!" And he did.

Mother was concerned that Ralph had already dropped out of school. Her concern was that he would have a hard time making a living. She really did not know why he was not in school. Neither did I, but I really didn't care. Each day he would drive by Coffee High at lunch time to see me. I would sit on the curb stone on the corner of Wood Avenue and Poplar Street. When I saw the Hoover truck, I'd turn my head. Silly, love struck girl who was only 16. We dated four months, without Mother's approval. Example of a no-win situation is the war time rules—all shades at home must be pulled at dark, because of potential air raids. Mother's rules were that I could not sit in the truck with Ralph after dark, yet I could not ask him in because the shades had to be pulled (just one of many little trials of life). At this time in our lives, Ralph and I were seriously considering marriage—what can we do? The Wilson family liked me, but thought we were too young. The best remedy was to get married, yet keep it a secret, even from Willa Jean.

Gentry & Gertie Wilson

After Ralph went to the court house and got a marriage certificate, stating that he was 21 and that I was 18, we told Mother we were going to Nashville to the Grand Ole Opry. Ralph came to the house to pick me up, borrowing his brother Elden's car and a coat. I wore a new black and white dress and had on my first nylon hose. We drove around for about an hour, then went to Killen, Alabama, and found a preacher's home and got married. The preacher had to call in a witness, so he asked his neighbor to come and witness the marriage. She recognized Ralph as one of Gentry Wilson's sons, but no one could tell on us because there was no phone there. Ralph took me home,

Lucille in her wedding dress

gave me the marriage certificate, and the game of "hiding the evidence" began. I put it between the mattress and springs of my bed. But every time Mother started to clean my room, I would slip it out and hide it under the sofa pillows. We were able to keep our secret for about a month, then one day that I should go to summer school, I was taking a needed history subject I needed for my first year at the University of Alabama. I told Robert while he was driving me to school that I had decided I wasn't going to school any more. He told me Mother would be mad; I replied, "I don't care, I don't have to go, I'm married." He turned the car around and back to 319 Middle Road we went. After lunch, Ralph drove up in his Hoover truck, got out and was having a short visit with me. We were sitting on the piano bench and who should come in, but Mother. I immediately told Mother about our marriage, not knowing what to expect. She came across the room and hugged us both, telling me how much she loved me and wishing us both complete happiness. From that moment on, she tried to help us get started in our married life.

Ralph rented us a furnished room and kitchenette next door to Poplar Street church of Christ. We had to share the bath with another couple. I was not prepared to keep house even though I had four years of home economics. I could not plan and cook a real meal. Our first grocery trip was a joke. We bought a pound of bacon, a dozen eggs, and a quart of milk, but no bread, no skillet, and no egg flip. But who cared, we were not far from the Wilson home, we'd eat a good supper with them. I had learned to make salmon patties; so the next day, Mother came to town and bought me some more groceries. I prepared salmon for my wonderful, loving husband. I learned that he does not eat salmon. So what? We'll go back to Mrs. Wilson's and eat again. I eventually learned to cook, and I was always a good housekeeper. Ralph did not want me to work outside the home; so I just stayed home and combed my "beautiful, long hair" that he so admired!

Throughout these years things were happening at Middle Road. Music had continued to be our "rock of Gibraltar". We had always had a piano, and it was always used. Even Robert stopped by the keys to play "Near You" with such great rhythm. The popular songs of the 40's were so beautiful, and Mother could give them a special beat that was uniquely hers. Her favorite popular hits were "Alexander's

Lucille & Ralph, 1942

Rag Time Band," "Sunrise Serenade," "Ma, He's Making Eyes at Me," "Chattanooga Shoe Shine Boy," "St. Louis Blues," "Top Smith's Boogie-Woogie."

Playing seemed to take her mind off all her cares. Her son was in the army, her mother was ill, she couldn't make production at the knitting mill, her baby boy was unable to cope with the cares of teenage life. But Mother loved her family, music, flowers, sewing, and knowledge. I think in that order. It was about this time that Mamahatha became ill with a stroke, and this time it was fatal. Once again, Mother was faced with a tragedy that seemed almost overwhelming. If only we had known how much she needed our strength and comfort at this time. Our Buddy knew. He asked for and received a time-off to come home for the funeral. The Nazarene Trio (Pearl and Lola Weatherford, and Addie Gray) and the Quillen Brothers (church of Christ) of Loretto, Tennessee, provided the music. I don't think any of us were aware of the strength Mamahatha had in holding her family together. After her death, everything seemed to disintegrate. Buddy was once again our hero. The one our family turned to when things looked bad, and the whole world was looking bad at this time.

The Wilson family welcomed me with open arms. I did notice that Mrs. Wilson cried so much. I wondered what I had done to cause her unhappiness. Years later I would understand the responsibility of marriage, and she knew what was ahead for us. The Wilson's had a large family—three girls and four boys. Ruth, the first daughter, worked in the payroll department of Flagg Knitting Company. Grace, the second daughter, was a private secretary to the president of Flagg Knitting, Mr. J. T. Flagg. James Elden, the oldest son, worked at Reynolds in accounting. Ralph Denson, my husband, had dropped out of school in the eighth grade because of surgery, and wanting to help the family financially worked driving a truck. Roy Glenn, Lonnie Lee, and Thelma Jewel were still in school. They were a wonderful Christian family who welcomed another daughter or sister. I have said so many times that the father Gentry, who was a supervisor at Flagg Knitting, was the finest Christian man I had ever met. Mrs. Gertie Lee Coker Wilson, the wife and mother fit the description of a godly woman found in Proverbs 31. I spent the first two years of my marriage visiting her, listening to her tell of her family, childhood, and how she met and married Gentry. I learned to cook the way she cooked and helped her in her planned weeks. She was very organized (had to be with nine people at home). Monday, she straightened the house and worked outside on flowers; Tuesday, she washed; Wednesday, ironed; Thursday and Friday, mended, quilted, and if any spare time embroidered pillow cases, etc. Saturday, each child at home had specific chores, dusting, mopping, etc. The house would be spotless. Then we females would walk to town every Saturday afternoon from the Wilson home on 126 North Royal Avenue, up Mobile Street and "shop" at Rogers, Ann's Hat Shop, and Sears. We visited with friends that were also "shopping", then back home. Sunday, everyone got up early and all went to Sunday school and church at Central Baptist in East Florence. Ralph and I had to go into class with "old" people—remember, we were married. I became involved in the music, playing the piano (when needed) and singing in the choir.

Mr. Alex & Mother

My first Christmas as Mrs. Ralph Wilson was exciting and yet sad to me. At this time we had found a larger apartment at the Richardson home on Tombigbee Street with Mrs. Will Richardson, a landlord who took us under her wing and was so very kind to us. Yet I still missed my family so much. Every time I heard the song "White Christmas," I'd think of my sweet older brother Buddy, and I'd cry myself sick. He had sent me a picture of him beside a little tent, and I knew what danger he was in. He served in four major battles, but God had plans for him to come home to Florence. My dear Mother brought Ralph and me a little cedar Christmas Tree for our new apartment. Mother put a cute doll, with a white tissue dress as an angel on the top of our little tree, and every year since 1942 it has been on my Christmas tree. My mother who lost her first husband, my daddy, in 1939, had met the second love of her life, Mr. Earl Alexander. While we were somewhat saddened by the marriage, we were happy that mother had found a new love and could find happiness again. Mr. Alexander was very kind to her and accepted Robert and Willa Jean into his home.

I was a happy wife, with such a loving husband. We had so many dreams and talked about our plans for the future, but Uncle Sam had plans for Ralph Denson Wilson—the draft. In the spring of 1943, he went into the army, a very unhappy nineteen year old. He hated being away from me, his family, and his home town. He never changed his feeling, even though he served his country. He was put into the truck driving and truck maintenance department of the Army in Fort Eustis, Virginia. He was so pleased to get a short furlough in July 1943.

I had divided my time, while Ralph was away, between Mother and Mr. Alex and the Wilsons. I would ride the Joiner Bus to Anderson and spend time with my own dear family. Willa Jean and I really enjoyed playing the piano together and Mother was so happy to show me around her home. We would attend Anderson Baptist Church. My time with the Wilsons was more solemn, because all four brothers were in service or getting ready to go.

After Ralph's furlough in 1943, he returned to Fort Eustis and became better adjusted, and finally decided to be content. He was later assigned totally as a machinist in the truck division. This became a burden for him and also a danger. While working on a fan belt replacement, he had all four fingers of his left hand amputated. So he came home unable to do many things, but he could still drive a truck. After Ralph was discharged from the army, we rented an apartment on Tombigbee Street in Florence. Mrs. Will Richardson was a wonderful, caring landlady.

Ralph & Lucille

Ralph & Lucille

1944 was a very memorable year as many events happened, some happy, yet some sad. In January Willa Jean informed us of her planned wedding. I wanted to be sure she had "something old, something new, something borrowed, something blue so I loaned her my hose that I wore when I got married, taking care of two of those important things for her. We had all learned to love James Cagle and felt sure he would always love and take care of her—which he really has for over 61 years. Another very important event was the birth of our first child, a healthy, beautiful, bouncing baby boy that we named Ralph Johnson Wilson, born April 24, 1944. We chose his name from his father Ralph and my maiden name Johnson. He was the first grandchild on both sides of our family, need I say more? I was visiting Mother and Mr. Alex when he decided that he was ready for his appearance into our busy world. Ironically, at this time Ralph was away on a Baggett trucking trip near Hoover Dam and did not return until his bouncing baby boy was about a week old. Mother and Mr. Alex took me to the nearest doctor and clinic at 5 a.m. which was Jackson Clinic in Lester, Alabama. I was blinded by high blood pressure and could not see Dr. Jackson until the next day after Ralph J. was born.

Ralph, Ralph J. & Lucille

All the aunts and uncles wanted to rock and swing him all the time. Ralph and I were fortunate to rent a cute little house about a block from the Wilson home which was so convenient since every time my baby would hold his breath, I could grab him up and run to my mother-in-law. This was quite often. He really wanted 100% of my attention, and he got it. Such a beautiful, sweet baby. Mother kept him in pretty clothes that she made for him. She and Mr. Alex made so many visits to our house, always bringing "goodies".

Mother also wrote so many special cards and letters to him—really, I'm not going to say he could read, but I read them to him, over and over. He was the first grandchild, so he gave the name of Mammy and Pop to Mother and Mr. Alex. These love names followed them all their lives. Mr. and Mrs. Wilson were Pap-paw and Grandmother.

It was after Ralph J.'s birth that I made my second commitment to the Lord—that I would always use my talent of music—piano, organ and voice—anytime I was asked. When I was only eight years old and going to Meridian Baptist Church I was very involved in the G.A.'s (Girls Auxiliary), girls mission group at church. No one could play our theme song, "We've a Story to Tell to the Nation." I prayed so much and so many times, "Lord, let me learn this song, and I'll never refuse to use my talent for You." Well, I learned it and played it all the time. I had rheumatic fever, leaving all fingers swollen and stiff after

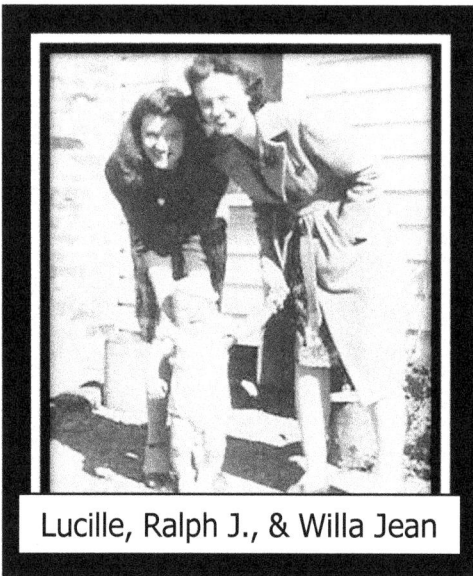
Lucille, Ralph J., & Willa Jean

Ralph J. was born, so I asked the Lord to help me again, and He did. I have now played for so many music functions: worship services, weddings, music groups, etc., even teaching music, and I have never yet charged for anything except the lessons I taught. God is so good.

Chapter 15: Willa Jean

And where were Willa Jean and Robert all this time? Waiting in the sidelines—just biding their time. It seems we always had something going. Once, for fun, we rode old Jack and the pony down Hough Road which started right about where our house was (see picture). After all the excitement of Sister's elopement, I was not sure I ever wanted to get married. Besides, Louise and I had already decided we were going to marry Gene Autry and Roy Rogers. Seriously, my second adventure into the halls of Coffee was being quite successful. After two years at St. Florian (8th and 9th grades), I was ready for 10th grade and Coffee Senior High School. Mr. Hibbett was still my principal, but, thankfully, no Hackworth was around, and I had friends who had transferred with me from St. Florian.

Willa Jean & Robert at Middle Rd. barn.

These halcyon days were about to end, however, for Mother had met our insurance salesman and had fallen in love for the first time since Daddy's death. Mr. Earl Alexander had been our insurance agent for quite a while, but Mother had not noticed him until just recently. Perhaps, all the excitement about Sister's marriage and Mamahatha's death had made her more vulnerable. Plus, she had become quite ill, lately. It began slowly at first, just slightly nauseous, then pale and sweaty. She couldn't get

Mr. Alex & Mother

out of bed. We called the doctor, and he said she was having a nervous breakdown. I knew something was badly wrong because as much as she loved music, she couldn't stand to hear me practice my French horn. I was now in the band at Coffee High School, but in order to practice, I had to go to the barn and play to Bessie and Jack, and even they didn't like it. Mother tried to be patient, but she was very sick. Mr. Alex was so understanding. He would bring groceries by, and he was such a good cook! He would not only buy the food, he would cook it, too! I was having a hard time trying to keep just the three of us together now. I not only had to do all the housework, I had old Bessie to tie out and try to milk. I also had to cook which I hated to do (and still do) and to help my little brother with his

Mother – After beautification.

homework. Mr. Alex seemed to be always around and so

House on Middle Rd.

very helpful. Mother's health seemed to be getting better, color was coming back into her cheeks, and Robert and I breathed sighs of relief. For the first time, we began to consider taking a "foreigner" into our Johnson home. He seemed to like the same things we liked—music, good food, outdoors, and Mother—not necessarily in that order. Sister and Ralph were also beginning to visit with us. Ralph was still driving a Hoover truck so Sister came when the truck and Ralph were available. Other times, she and Ralph came out in his brother Elden's car. Buddy, who was stationed overseas at this time, wrote to Mother almost daily, and Mother also wrote to him. We all sent frequent letters as can be seen in the appendix (letters). Mother tried to make our home as attractive as she could. Although there were no marble works to beautify our home, we had beautiful plants (see pictures before and after).

I don't think I have mentioned anything about my love life since my chauffeurs (Ralph and Sis) deserted me. So here goes! I met this young man—completely blonde (I think he was an albino)—at Milner Rushing. Robert and I were going to a western show on Saturday afternoon. This young man offered to take me home (which I refused). He then asked if he could come to see me. I saw no reason why not, so I said yes. However, by the next Saturday, I was a nervous wreck. When his car drove up (chauffeured by his dad), he got out of the car with a box of candy, and I panicked! I couldn't go to the door, so guess what! I hid! I have always been ashamed. If I could have remembered his name, I would have apologized, but I had no idea. Robert had one more tale to hold over my head. But at least he couldn't say I tried to drown myself! (As he did in the episode about the house by the pond)

Robert and I were slowly winning our war with words in persuading Mother to become Mrs. Alexander.

(There was so much we didn't know at this time that I will relate at a later time in this book.) She was so very tired of not making production at the knitting mill, counting pennies, and rationing books. She yearned for the days when she could stay at home and play her beloved piano all day or work in her flower garden. How she wished for this hateful war to be over and for her oldest son to be back with her once again! While Mr. Alex was certainly not the answer to all these wishes, he seemed to be holding out a helping hand toward a solution for some of them.

After the decision was made to marry, things began to start moving at a swifter pace. The wedding took place in mid-January 1943--at the end of our first semester at Coffee and St. Florian, respectively. We only had time to gather our belongings and move to a place we had never seen before. Mother and Mr. Alex had spent the week-end before preparing the house for us, and they drew us a map on how to get there. Robert (naturally) drove. He was 13. From Rogersville we went down Snake Road, which was unpaved, and then turned off on Ridge Road. Old Spot was in the back seat, and I expected him to howl at any minute. Dust was boiling around the car, and there were only a few houses. I thought Robert had lost the way, and I was ready to get back at him about "getting lost" when he said he thought he saw Mr. Alex's car! It's hard to describe how I felt when I first saw the house at New Georgia. I wanted to cry. I was sure we had come to the end of the earth. There couldn't be much else. Then I saw the slanted pine tree in the front yard. It fascinated me. I'm sure there were so many stories about that tree, and it looked just right to climb up in and read a good book! So we crawled out, dusted off our clothes, and entered a brand new life at New Georgia in Rogersville, Alabama.

We arrived at New Georgia on Saturday, unpacked a few things, but were unprepared for a good old-fashioned country welcome the very next day! At least it was a welcome from the teenagers of the community. The adults would come crawling out later. We didn't go to church that Sunday and were just relaxing when a car came whizzing by our front porch! I didn't see all the occupants. I was too interested in the one with dark hair and eyes, white shirt, and sleeveless sweater. I was sure he did not see me. He was much too old to be interested in a 15 year old. But, wow! I really think he did look at me. After all, there were no more girls standing on my porch. Other teenagers walked up to see us from Mr. Moody's farm next door. Mr. Moody was my future husband's grandfather. Catherine Cagle, James' sister, was the first person I officially met in New Georgia. Maybe that is why I love her so now. She has always been such a dear friend. All the Cagle's have been, but I am getting ahead of myself.

After all the dust settled on that romantic Sunday afternoon, the next day was Monday, the first day of a new semester at a new school—Lauderdale County High School. I got on the bus at the home next door to ours (another Moody, Johnny Mac, uncle of James); and away I went toward an uncharted course. But guess what! James, that good-looking guy, got on the bus and sat by me--actually talked to me. I was speechless! The rest of that day went by in a blur, and now I knew what Sister meant when she talked about love at first sight! He saved me a seat on the bus that afternoon. That did it! There was never another man in my life.

My little brother did not fare quite as well. Anderson Junior High was not his cup of tea. After all, Robert had been through so very much in his short life, and so many of these children were still "children". Some of his best friends were people my age. For example, he had a huge crush on Catherine, James' sister, who was my age. Since he couldn't cope with the situation as it was at school,

Willa Jean & James

Robert simply joined the Navy. He found it quite easy to change his age when necessary since he looked older than he actually was, and, since the Navy needed more young men, he had no trouble getting in. Later in life, Robert told us he used to tell people he attended school at Alabama—they accepted that. He never explained that he meant Anderson, Alabama. I'm not sure how long Robert stayed in the Navy before they found out about his age! He did, however, get an honorable discharge from the Navy. He must have turned directly around and joined the Air Force. We are not sure how long this term lasted.

Mother, in the meantime, was looking after her children, as usual. When she found out that Mr. Roy Harrison, principal at Anderson school, had whipped Robert with a belt buckle, she proceeded to have him (the principal) demoted right away. No one was going to hurt her children! However, she was also beginning to see some of her dreams come true. She was teaching piano lessons, attending all day singings, working in her flowers, and sewing for the underprivileged. If she could only get Robert settled and Buddy back home.

Mr. Alex, Mother, James, Mama Cagle, Grandaddy

Things were going quite well with James Cagle and me. At least I thought so, until I saw him pass my house with another girl! I thought my heart would break. At least he tried to hide, but I declared my undying unforgiveness for him. We later met in the school library, and he passed me a note asking me to marry him! Naturally, I refused!! (at least for the time being) James was in the senior class school play, and I fell in love with him all over again. Coming back from the play, we saw a falling star. He said that meant he could steal a kiss, and so he did. He also told me that he was going into the Air Force. Suddenly, all the above trite little things were as nothing. What was important was James was going to serve his country, perhaps even give his life, and I was worried about little things! I'm not sure this was the exact date, but it was about this time that he and I talked for hours about many things that were important to both of us. Later, he let me guide his car, and, as we were still engrossed in heavy conversation, we left the road and ended up a ditch, a pretty deep one at that. It was too late to try to get someone out to help us out so we had to walk home, about 2 miles (from James' daddy's home to Mother's home). We woke Mother, and James who still had marriage on his mind asked her for my hand in marriage. I think Mother was so sleepy, she didn't actually know what was going on so she said okay. Poor James had to walk or maybe he ran all the way back to his house, got his mules and pulled his car out of the ditch. I wonder if he knew just what he was asking for.

I received my engagement ring on my 16th birthday. I was in the 11th grade and had every intention of completing my education. We had planned to get married in June of 1944. The Army can work in mysterious ways, however. When we found out that James was going to be sent overseas, we decided to move our wedding date up to January 24, 1944. During my semester break, I went out to Amarillo, Texas, where James was stationed. I bought my bus tickets through Joiner's Bus Line. When I got about half way out, I found out that the tickets were only good through Arkansas. I didn't have enough money with me to pay for the rest, so they (the bus people) gave me the tickets. (People were kind-hearted to service personnel.) But, instead of getting into the bus station as scheduled at about 9 p.m., I arrived at about 2 a.m.   Poor James was asleep in the terminal. I was absolutely terrified—of James, of the buses, of all the noise, of everything. All I wanted was to be at home with my mother. When I looked at James, I was not even sure I knew him. I had worn my Jodhpurs and boots on the trip out there, and I dreaded changing into a skirt and stockings (Sister had loaned me her hose). Sure enough, I couldn't keep them up. (But that's another story.) I suddenly felt 16 years old, not grown-up at all. I had never been away from home before. Everything that had happened to my family for the past 4 or 5 years started flashing before my eyes, and I felt as though I were dreaming, and I wanted to wake up. Except there was James, there were those brown eyes looking at me past

the bus window, and when he smiled, I saw the sweet dimples on his face; I knew I hadn't made a mistake. So I slipped my boots back on (yes, my feet hurt, even back then), tightened my belt, got off the bus and faced a new life. Mr. and Mrs. James Cagle were married on the top floor of the courthouse in Amarillo, Texas, and every time I would move, my stockings would fall down. I felt so sorry for James. I know he

James & Willa Jean

was embarrassed. He had met me at the bus station at 2:00 in the morning, but we had to wait until he court house opened at 9 a.m. to get married. We stayed in the guest house on the base. I had a new beige suit I was so proud of. Sis had loaned me her silk hose. Louise had given me a great big scare about married life, so I was all set. We had exactly ten days to enjoy our honeymoon. Then I had to get back to my 11th grade books, and James back to his Air Force studies. He was working on electrical systems for the B-29's. We thought there would be enough time for us to be together later in the year. Little did we know what the future would hold for us! Our time was cut short when they told James he would be shipped out to Canute Field in Illinois. So I had to pack up my bags and head back home.

Even though 1944 was a banner year for me, one I will never forget, there were also tragedies in this year. We learned directly after returning from my marriage that Aunt Elsa, one of my very favorite aunts in Knoxville, had passed away of tuberculosis.

The Cagle Clan

None from our family was able to go to the funeral because of the gas rationing. It was also in the spring of 1944 that Sister's husband, Ralph, had the terrible accident in camp and lost four fingers on his left hand.

The Cagle family was so kind and understanding to me while James was away. I know now that we were truly the "new folks" in town, and they didn't have to open up their arms in that way, but they did—to me, to Robert, and to Mother also. We were blissfully unaware that Mr. Alex had only recently divorced his first wife, Zaddie, and that the community was really down on him because of this divorce. We had something to prove, even though we were unaware of it at the time. Mother continued her good work of helping the sharecroppers who were working on Mr. Alex's farm, and Robert and I went right on with our lives. My marriage to James, who was a member of one of the oldest families in the community, must have helped, but we were not aware of any stigma we might have had. Sis and I later discussed the unusual format of our in-law families. James was the 2nd son; so was Ralph. There were seven children in each household; four boys and three girls. We could go on and on, but I would like to stop here to introduce my in-laws. Mr. Cagle, the patriarch who came to see me on his horse on an almost daily basis after I became pregnant with my first child. Mama Cagle, who was in many ways so much like Mother and yet so different, had long beautiful black hair, and would you believe, she and Mother had also dated the same boy as teenage girls, yet they had never met? They became close friends after James and I got married. Mildred, the oldest daughter, was the boss of the family and loaned James enough money for us to get married. E. F., who spent four years away from his family while in the army, was stationed in England. He lost a baby son, but was not even able to come back to the funeral. Eugene, almost a twin to James, was just 15 months younger. He was in my room at school and was very smart. Catherine, like a sister to me, still, was a hard worker whom Robert had a crush on. Billy Ray, the last little boy, about Robert's age but who seemed so much younger, had pretty brown eyes like James'. He was later in the Korean War, I think. Little Shirley, who was a late in life baby, was beautiful, spoiled and sweet. If you have ever read Little Women, she would fit the role of Amy. This many children (7)—and yet they welcomed more. By this time, E.F. was married to Willie T. Goodman, so there were 8 and I made 9. Mama Cagle and Grandaddy made 11. We all sat around a long table with a Home Comfort stove holding a big coffee pot and a pan of Mama Cagle's biscuits when I surprised them all!

We were going to be 12. James and I became pregnant during one of his leaves home in the Spring of 1944. I continued my school year in the 11th grade, but did not complete the 12th since I was expecting my first child in March of 1945.

James & his horse

Chapter 16: Johnsons – 1944

1944 was a very busy year for all of us. It was a banner year in that Willa Jean got married, Robert went to the army (again), Sister had her first child, and Buddy was landing in Angio's Beachhead. He was in four major battles which changed his life forever. Regardless of how busy he was, however, or how confused he was about what all was happening to his family back home, he never forgot to write. He kept up correspondence with Aunt Elise, Ruth Wilson, and all the immediate family giving us instructions on what to do and how to do it. If he couldn't get birthday cards, he made them up and wrote beautiful poems to his sisters back home. (See appendix)

Even though Mother did no farming on her own, she loved living on the farm, she could spent hours working in her flowers and sewing to her heart's content. She spend hours making clothes for tenant farmers' families. She even delivered a baby in one of the farmers' homes, and the child was named after her. Mother was very kind and gentle to all she met as long as they were kind and gentle in turn, but they had better not ever try to take advantage of her or of hers for she knew how to take care of herself.

Mother loved to go with Mr. Alex on his insurance routes for she studied her music while she was riding with him. One week-end they went away and left Robert and Willa Jean at home to pick the remainder of the cotton and store it in the loft of the barn. Well, they picked for a while, then threw the bags of cotton up in the barn. They had heard that cotton wouldn't burn, so they tried it. It didn't burn—at least not until about midnight. The next morning when they woke up, there was no barn. Mr. Alex never asked them to pick any more cotton.

Sister and "Little" Ralph visited with Mother many times while Ralph was gone on truck trips. Robert was in and out of the service, but Willa Jean got to play with the sweetest little baby in the world. Little Ralph had such a good nature and was happy to be with anyone. Mother and Mr. Alex continued their out-of-town trips, and Willa Jean and Sister cleaned house for Mother burning this time, not cotton and barns, but old purses and anything else we thought Mother would not miss. However, we couldn't seem to make a dent. We always ended up playing the piano and singing—just as we still do today.

Mother at New Georgia home

Chapter 17: 1945 - Willa Jean

The spring of '45 brought the first granddaughter into the Johnson family. Carolyn was born to Willa Jean and James on March 19, 1945. On that unforgettable Sunday afternoon, we had had many visitors at Mother's home— Paul and Ollie, the entire Cagle clan, and cousins from the Moody family. They all wanted to see the pretty clothes in the trunk which we had covered in pretty baby wallpaper on the Saturday before. I had received an official document from the Air Force telling me not to worry if I didn't hear from James for some time. He would be safe! Naturally, I panicked! And did exactly the opposite from what I was supposed to do. I thought he had been taken a prisoner, or worse, was killed in action. I was terrified! I think that was when my back first started hurting.

Carolyn, 6 weeks

Carolyn & Ralph J.

James & Willa Jean

By the time the visitors had all left, I was exhausted, swollen, and tired. Mother and Mr. Alex put away everything, and I retired, I thought, for the night. But, oh no! Carolyn had decided today was the day! My feet were so swollen I had to wear Mr. Alex's overshoes. Mother, Mr. Alex, and I packed my bags and raced by New

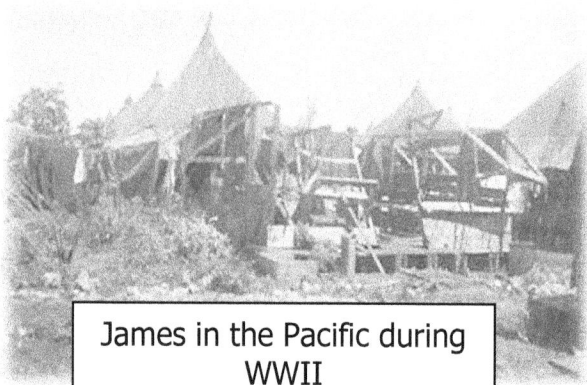

James in the Pacific during WWII

Georgia church, which had just turned out services for the evening, and we headed for Dr. Jackson's clinic where our little Ralph had been delivered about 11 months earlier.

The Cagles were just headed home with Eugene driving his car ahead of us. We tooted the horn, the motor died, and I was on the back seat lying down when the seat fell out in the floor! Eventually, however, we made it to the hospital, where, after about 6-8 hours later, a beautiful little black-haired baby girl was delivered—

James in the Pacific during WWII

Carolyn Jean Cagle, 7 lbs,2 oz.. Granddaddy Cagle called her a little Japanese. We stayed in the hospital 7 days. We sent a cablegram to James about the birth of his baby, but he never received it, since he was on a ship, going from India across to the Pacific Ocean to the Mariana Islands.

He only heard of her birth about two months later when he received a letter with a picture of a 3 week old baby (see picture).

At the time of Carolyn's birth, James was being relocated from India to the Mariana Islands where he remained until the end of the war. He was on the

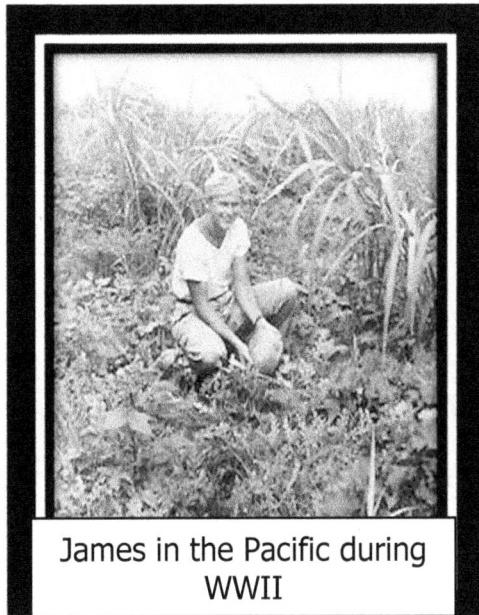

James in the Pacific during WWII

island where the planes took off from to bomb Hiroshima.

Chapter 18: 1945 – Lucille

Our next move was to an apartment on Mobile Street. I was also expecting a baby at this time. We were not able to determine the sex of a child back then so we all thought this one would be a girl. But what a gorgeous surprise! First of all, he was born 2 months early and weighed only 4 lbs 10 oz. He was a beautiful, tiny, brown-eyed little boy who could look straight through you!

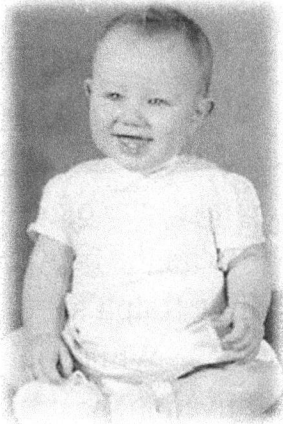

Ralph J.

James D. (Denny)

James Denson Wilson was born June 16, 1945, at ECM Hospital. He was named for two uncles James Wilson and James Cagle. Denson was his father's name. Years before, his great-grandfather was named James Denson. Mr. Alexander was also there to take me to the hospital.

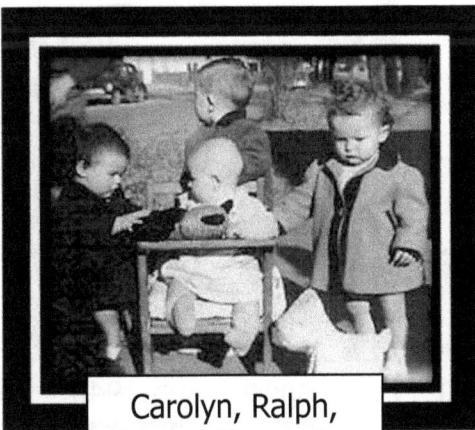

Carolyn, Ralph, Denny, Jimmy Joe

Mother went straight home and made some tiny little gowns to fit a tiny little baby. She cut some of Ralph's diapers into four pieces so that they would be small enough for Denny. While I was still in the hospital with my tiny, robust son, James Denson, Ralph took our oldest son Ralph Johnson, for his first overnight visit with his grandparents, Mr. and Mrs. Gentry Wilson, who brought him back to be with us the day I came home. He dearly

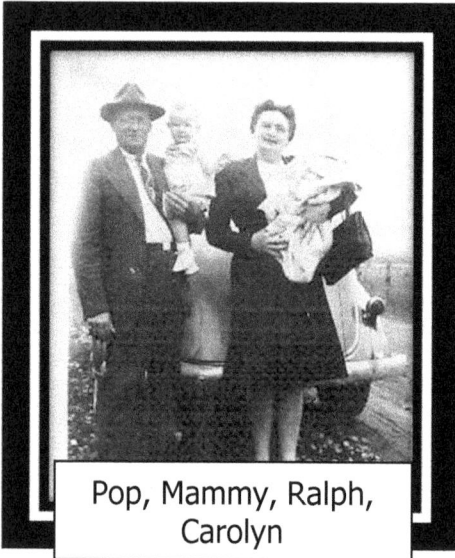

Pop, Mammy, Ralph, Carolyn

loved his "bajgy", but didn't want to give up his right to his own little bed! It was a very busy spot by my bedside with a bassinet pulled up to take care of the tiny baby and the baby bed to rub little Ralph's "back! back!!!". While Ralph and I lived in the Terrell's upstairs apartment, Lorraine Terrell was truly a life saver.

She saw and fully understood the trying times that I was going through since she also had two babies within thirteen months of each other. Lorraine had three boys –Charles, Billy, and Bobby. When "Little Ralph" would wake up during the night and cry, Lorraine would come to my rescue. She came up the stairs

Prospect Street 1946

and slipped him out, taking him downstairs and putting him in bed with her and her husband. They were so very helpful.

Mobile Street 1945

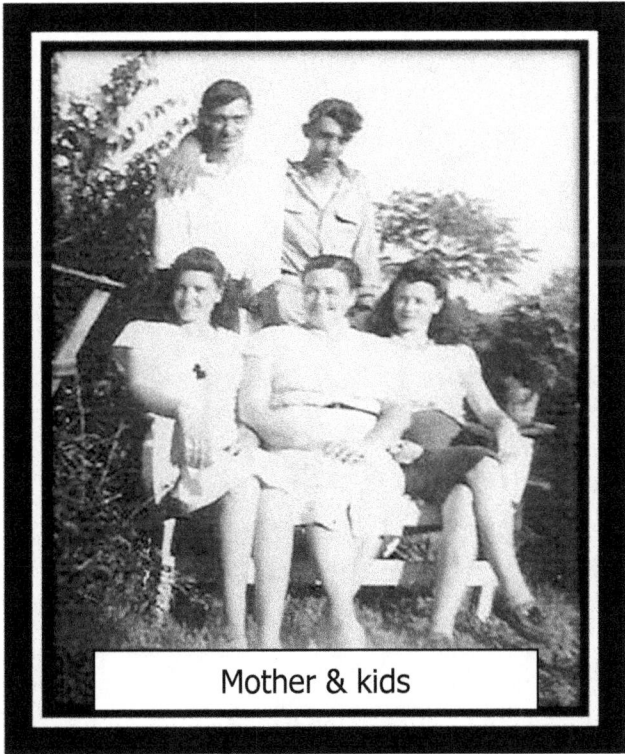

Mother & kids

Chapter 19: 1945 - Willa Jean and Lucille

How busy we all were—babies, babies, babies, and we were not finished yet! In the midst of all of our personal happiness, there was national happiness too! Our country was at peace once again. V-Day, June 1945, all our boys were on their way home again. James had not

Ralph, Lucille, Ralph J. & Denny

been home since Willa Jean was pregnant so he had not seen Carolyn.

Buddy came home in July, E.F. in June. After a few days of happy reunion with Mother, Willa Jean, Carolyn, and new step father, Mr. Alex, Buddy settled in with Sister, Ralph and their two boys on Mobile Street to be closer to school. He had to sleep on a roll-a-way bed in Sister's kitchen at night, but who cares, he was accustomed to bed in a tent. We were so happy to have our sweet brother home.

The nation had a new policy which was great for our soldiers! The government paid for schooling for vets who wished to continue their education. Buddy lost no time

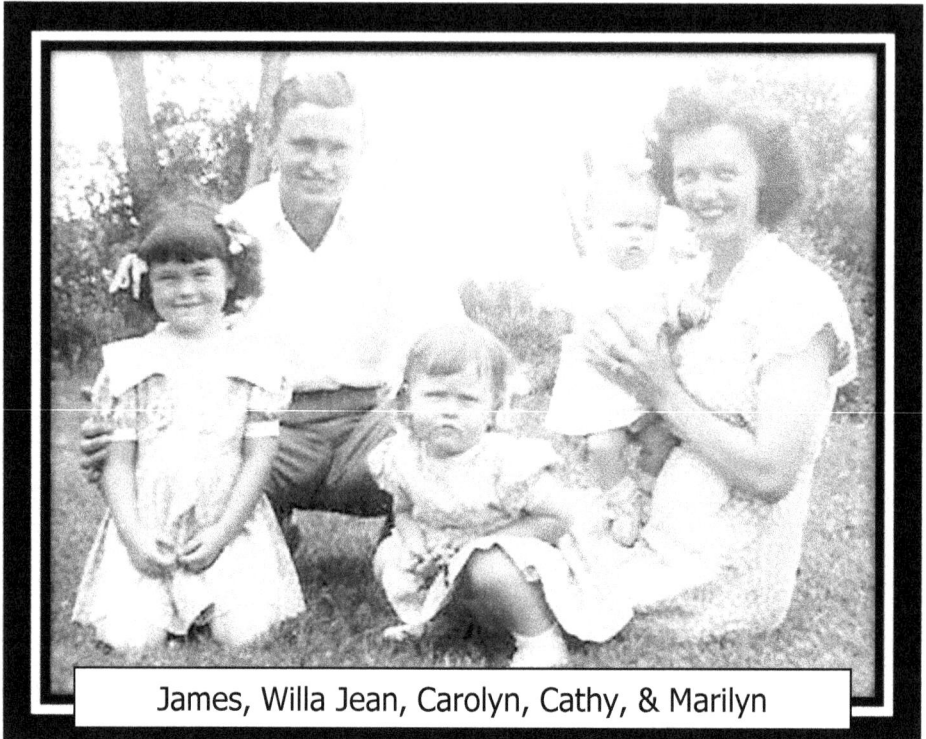

James, Willa Jean, Carolyn, Cathy, & Marilyn

taking advantage of this opportunity. His plans were to be a teacher coach. He enrolled at Florence State in early September and was instrumental in organizing the first drum and bugle corps which later became the Florence State College band.

It was at this time, as Buddy and Ralph were walking down Court Street that they met a beautiful blond. Buddy remarked, "What a gorgeous blond." Ralph asked, "Would you like to meet her?" Buddy's reply was, "Sure!" That was the last of the dark haired Parisian beauty who had played such a significant role in our brother's life during the war. From that day forward Buddy and Jo Marie Scott were as one. They married in October 1945.

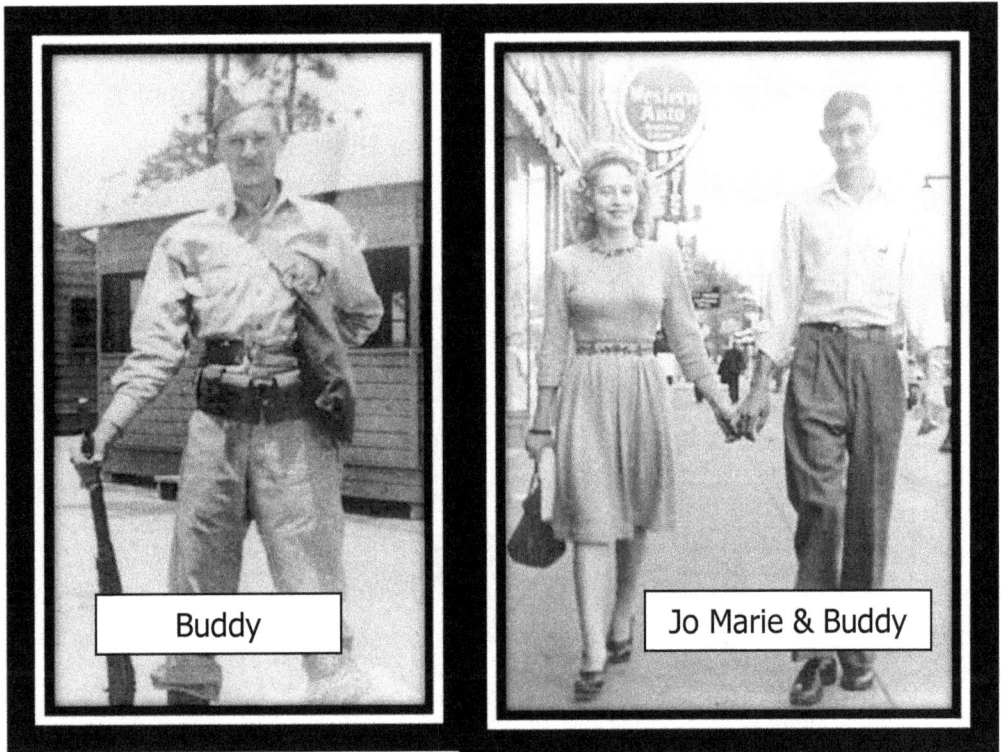

Buddy

Jo Marie & Buddy

At this time, our baby brother Robert was still in service. Willa Jean was living with both the Cagle's and Pop and Mother. She was still in high school, trying desperately to complete her education since James had promised Mother he would see that she finished high school. Carolyn was breast-fed so Willa Jean had to take classes that would allow her to be at home every four hours. It was highly unusual for young mothers to be in school, and the administration did not take this situation lightly, but you know our Mother! So Willa Jean attended school. However, she had to drop out of all her extracurricular activities, including Beta Club, Tri-Hi-Y, etc. Not that it mattered to her, especially when she heard that the war was almost over and that James was on his way home! He had not seen Carolyn! Carolyn was a walking, talking baby doll. She thought her daddy was an 8x11 picture, and she adored him. How disappointed she was when she saw this great big hulk of a guy (her mother thought was so handsome) who tried to kiss her! She tried to get away from him. To add insult to injury, he got her place in bed the very first night he came home. She had a baby bed, which she had never used, at Mama Cagle's house. She always slept with her mother and her Aunt Catherine. So homecoming was a little traumatic to say the least. This didn't last long, however, for everyone was so happy to see all the service men back home again. There was so much excitement and turmoil during this time that it was quite impossible for Willa Jean to attend school full-time, care for a baby, and be a full-time wife. So school had to go! James got a job in Florence ; so once again Willa Jean dropped out of school. This time with only two ½ courses to go, one semester each in English and social studies. Mother's dream of having her children walk across the stage for a diploma was still to be in the future. James came home from the Army with a good trade as an electrician, but jobs were not that plentiful. While outwardly everyone was at peace, inwardly, our boys who had been in service were suffering post-war syndrome and were nervous and extremely hard to get settled down to everyday living.

Robert

Chapter 20: Willa Jean 1946-1953

I had furnished a sweet little house down below the Cagle farm house while James was away. It had 3 rooms, a bedroom, living room, and kitchen. Naturally, the first piece of furniture I bought was a piano. Everything else fit around that and a baby bed, of course, which had never been used until James came home. It was then used very reluctantly by Carolyn who was 8 months old at that time.

Carolyn

There was no water in the house; so water was carried from Mama Cagle's house. No indoor plumbing, no outdoor either for that matter, only the woods! It was pretty scary and very isolated, but beautiful down there. James, Carolyn and I loved it there until James got his first job at Cockrell Electric. Then we moved to Florence into an apartment owned by Mother and Mr. Alexander on Prospect Street, near the college.

We had one large room on the ground floor and shared the bath (we really had indoor plumbing again!) with the rest of the tenants. When the room was made-up, with everything in place, it was beautiful. The couch made a bed, the make-believe radio was a gas stove. Everything had its place, but there was no place for a baby bed or baby toys! My mother didn't care, but the other tenants were not that kind, so I had to be very watchful. Sister later lived in the same building and her outlook was completely different from mine. So I guess it was just the way you look at certain things, or the way you feel when you are living there. We were never happy there. James really wanted to live in the country. So did I. Carolyn would live anywhere that she could be near her two grandmothers. She talked constantly, walked and felt confined in the one little room. So it was not long before we moved back to the country. This time we moved to an old house that was at one time Mama Cagle's old home place. It was now owned by Thecla and Ershel Teague, Mama Cagle's youngest sister. She was thrilled that we had rented this old house. It is the same one we have pictures of now in most of our homes. We celebrated Carolyn's first birthday here in this old house. There are many other fond memories here. Her first Easter egg hunt, first birthday party, and first ride on a cotton sack. I had some of my first here also. I had my first scare with a hoot owl! I was hanging out diapers (after dark) and heard this horrifying noise! I don't think my feet touched the ground. I fled back into the house and vowed never to return to that woody backyard again! But I did, over and over again! On another occasion, I was scrubbing my floors (I didn't have rugs or screen doors), a rooster came into my kitchen and stood up on my flour bin. He actually dared me to enter my own kitchen, and I didn't take his dare. I ran. Coward that I am, I think I grabbed my child. She was not the coward that I am. Years later, when tearing down the old house, we found Carolyn's hospital bracelet in the walls of the house. I don't know how it could have gotten there. Maybe in my mad rush to get outside? Or could she have been trying to stay behind? We truly had some memorable times at that old house.

James had decided he could make more money by making a cotton crop; so he bought two mules. We built a barn and fence and thought we had it made! But the mules were smarter than we were. When we were not looking, they jumped our fence and ended up in Salem. Alabama, that is! Sugar Creek bottom. Grandaddy helped James round the mules up, but when he (Grandaddy) tried to catch one of them, he fell into the creek, lost his shoe, and I don't remember how he ever got back. There are so many fond memories!

In the meantime, Mother and Mr. Alex had built a garage apartment at the back of their farm house on New Georgia road, and Buddy and Jo moved in there with their baby Janet. Janet was born in August of 1946 in Florence. Buddy taught school at Anderson. Mother and Mr. Alex attended church at Anderson Baptist Church while James and I continued to go to New Georgia church of Christ, driving back and forth even when living in Florence. I had been attending worship services with James' family at New Georgia Church of Christ while he was in the

Willa Jean, Lucille & children

service and had grown quite accustomed to that form of worship. I was even quite fond of singing with no musical instruments. I truly felt a closeness with God when I saw the congregation participating in weekly communion services.

Not long afterward, James and I were expecting our second child, Cathy. We decided to move back to the small cottage on the farm with Mama Cagle and Grandaddy. The one piece of furniture we always seemed to have was a piano which made everyone dread seeing us move. Meanwhile, Sister, Ralph and boys moved into the ground floor of Mother's apartment house on Prospect Street. Denny, a growing toddler, liked to play in the front yard, and the neighbors would come out just to watch him play. We are not sure if it was his big brown eyes, or his bald head, or his long gowns, but nevertheless he was fascinating. We all loved to meet at Mother's house with all our babies. Once, when we were all together, Buddy and I decided to drive to Anderson. We took the oldest grandchild, Little Ralph, with us. On the return trip, Little feisty Ralph kept trying to open the back door of the car which he succeeded in doing. Thank the good Lord, we were in a car with the doors opening from the front to the back. We didn't even hear the door open. We only saw a little white jumper with a little boy inside, sitting on the side of the road! This is a picture that we will never forget! He came stumbling up to meet us and we went back to Dr. Bayles at Anderson, got a few stitches along with the scratches and bruises and loads of tears! Sister met us half-way back home. Her instincts had already told her that something was wrong. Nothing was seriously wrong with our little boy, but it was a scare we would never forget. Oh, to have had car seats in 1946!

While we were busy with babies, bottles, burping, and bumping, Mother continued with her music. We all had pianos, even if we didn't have the time to play them. Mother always said we should take the time. After all, what is time, anyway? She didn't believe in clocks. She refused to have clocks in her house. Mother continued her dream of teaching music

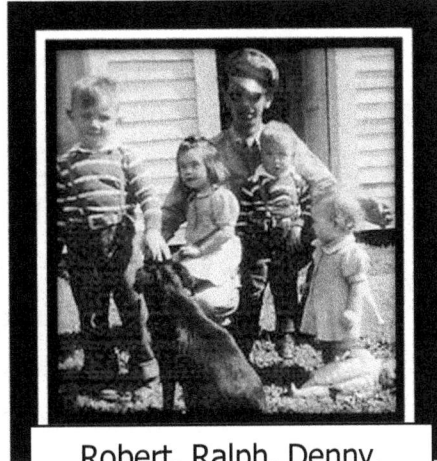

Robert, Ralph, Denny, Carolyn & Cathy

after she married Mr. Alexander. One of her first students was Shelva Jean Corum, who still lives in this area. Mother taught piano music at home and also at Anderson Junior High School.

In the meantime, James, Carolyn and I had decided farming was not our cup of tea after all. Our dilemma was that we wanted the country, but we wanted the money that went with city jobs! We compromised by moving back to our little house next to Mama Cagle and Grandaddy's farm (rent-free) and James started driving a milk truck. That was an adventure in and of itself! It was also about this time that we found out to our delight that we were expecting a new

James, Willa Jean & girls

little baby! Life was so full of surprises! So we redecorated our little house, happily moved our piano again, along with the rest of our furniture and eagerly awaited our new birth. This time we only casually notified Dr. Bayles of Anderson that we were expecting sometime in the spring. I suppose so he would not be shocked to be called out after dark? We went merrily on our way. Oh, to be young again! We were 18 and 21, and we knew everything (at least, almost everything). James had to get up about 4:00 every morning to go on his milk route, Carolyn and I would see him off and go back to bed, but our day began at daybreak when I carried water back down the hill to my house for washing, etc. The days became very long indeed. We had neither electricity nor running water (no bathrooms, showers, etc.) One of my hardest jobs was washing lamp globes. They are so fragile. I don't know how many I broke nor how many more I threatened to break. Mama Cagle had two Aladdin lamps. They were so gorgeous! Her house seemed so well lighted. I worked very hard to keep my lamp globes clean so we could read at night. I always kept books by our bed and couch. (Still do!) I'm sure my children and grandchildren can understand now just how precious books are to us.

1946 was an exceptionally cold winter. We had a number of snow days. As the time drew nearer for the birth of our second child, we knew that we could not stay in our little house for the event; first, because of the lack of heat, and second, because of the lack of water in the house. So we moved in with Mama Cagle and Grandaddy, much to Carolyn's delight. She dearly loved to be pampered by her aunts and uncles, and she had plenty of them. Catherine,

Eugene, Billy Ray, and Shirley were all still living at home, and Mildred came home every week-end; so did E.F. and Willie T, at least, almost every week-end; so the house was always filled to the brim with love and laughter.

There was not much to do for entertainment in the forties except for battery-operated radios, or just sitting around talking, or the most popular of all in our family— playing "Rook". Rook cards were expensive, though, so we made them from cardboard, carefully cutting out each section and coloring them yellow, black, red, and green, drawing the old rook a different color and everyone got set to go! Mama Cagle dearly loved to play rook. She looked over our shoulders at everyone's hand and tried to signal colors when she could catch our eyes! I think of these good old days every time we have a "snow on the ground" season! It was such a peaceful time. Everyone loved everyone else and no one seemed to care that there was not a late model car in the drive or that no one had a high paying job! We were all well and happy and snug in Mama Cagle's little farm house; so what could possibly go wrong? I don't remember if this event was the night before Cathy's birth, but I think it was. It was a very cold night and most of the Cagle's were home, playing rook as usual, with the tables and chairs pulled as close to the red-hot stove as possible. Grandaddy had already gone to bed (in the same room where we were playing cards). Carolyn was put to bed in the little side room adjoining the "master" bedroom with only a curtain separating the rooms. The house was old, but well kept. It did have room for occasional mice or rats from the barns, however. There was one hole under the staircase that one rat loved to try to escape from occasionally. James was watching that night and playing rook at the same time. When the rat looked out, James got a clear shot, then went right on bidding on his rook hand. I don't think the rifle shot woke Grandaddy nor Mama Cagle. They were used to the escapades of their sons. The night was long, and long after everyone else had retired, Cathy decided it was her time to enter into the Cagle clan. James and I had borrowed Catherine's room next to Mama Cagle and Grandaddy, and Carolyn was peacefully asleep there at that time. She and Shirley, who had been sleeping in the room with Mama Cagle and Grandaddy and all the noise of the rook game, were retired to the bedroom across the hall where the rest of the Cagle family awaited Cathy's birth. Grandaddy hurriedly made a fire in his "warm morning" kitchen stove and started boiling water. (I never understood before this time what boiling water was for at a birth.) Mamma Cagle insisted I move to her bed, so we changed the bed linens, and I moved to the extremely, overly warm room, which had just had the murdered rat, and James left (on foot, since he had just sold our last car the day before) to get Roxy Springer to help Mama Cagle and to get Mother (oh, and to get the doctor). I think Tonis Springer took him to Anderson to get Dr. Bayles. All this time, I was having back pains, but mainly I was worried about what was happening to my child across the hall. How could she sleep? There had to be at least five, maybe six or more Cagle's over there, but I couldn't hear a sound. I think they were trying to hear a sound out of me, but I refused to accommodate them. Things began to heat up about 5:00 in the morning. The water was boiling in the kitchen, and I was hurting in the bedroom. Cathy was waiting to be born.

Mother was fit to be tied, and the Doctor was still not there! He finally arrived, with some ether, which was truly appreciated, and with James' help (he helped soothe the cramps away), I was delivered of a beautiful, plump, cherub, pink and white, a dimpled and darling baby girl. Grandaddy had rigged up some cotton scales, and he tied a diaper across them and, would you believe, Cathy did not cry when she was weighed in at 6 lbs? Those Cagles across the hall were also in for a surprise when they found out she had already been born, and they had not heard any screams or yells! (Except those of Mother's!) It must have been very hard on Mother to see her daughter be so primitive. James and I both should have apologized to her for all the pain we put her through. And yet, when we think of what gorgeous children we had— and how proud she was of them— perhaps that was all the reward she wanted or needed.

Cathy

Well, maybe a few more rewards needed to be handed out. The baby had to be named. Cathyrn, after her Aunt Catherine, and Joyce, after her Uncle Eugene's girl friend. At the time, we didn't know we would be using names that would be needed later for their own children.

We only stayed at Mama Cagle's for five days after Cathy's birth. I didn't realize at the time how much trouble I would be for her and for the family, but as soon as I could get up and around, I took my little family back down to our little "dream" house in the woods. Mother begged us to stay with her, but Mr. Alexander wanted her with him on his insurance route, and James truly wanted to stay in his own home so home we went! And it worked out just great. Except, of course, we carried our water from the main house (Mama Cagle's) since we had no plumbing facilities, and it was coooooold!!! Regardless, my babies flourished. Carolyn was a doll, even when she pretended Cathy was one. Cathy was an angel (still is), caused no trouble, except when she was hungry or wet. However, one warm morning when I decided my children needed to enjoy the bright sunlight, I rolled my baby carriage out on the front porch and left Carolyn outside playing while I watched and worked inside. I heard my baby screaming and ran outside to see that her precious little face was covered with black bumble bees!! I had put the carriage in front of a bumble bee nest! I had to rush her to Dr. Bayles again. I can't remember my transportation this time. James was on the milk route. Cathy had been stung in a number of places on her face, but, thankfully, none of the stings were life-threatening.

I was almost ready to give up and say this country life is not for me! But I decided to wait just a while longer. A few weeks later, I got up with James as he prepared to leave on his milk route. I heard his truck go down Mince Creek hill, but instead of slowing down, it just kept going faster and faster. His brakes had given way, and he wrecked his truck, hurting his back. This was the pits! Soon after he recovered from this accident, he was offered an opportunity to return to armed service, with a guarantee that he would not be sent overseas. We didn't hesitate. All our adults were against this decision, but we thought we knew better. So we signed up and away we went for another term in the Army Air Force. This time we were stationed in Selma, Alabama, and this time, I could go with James and take the two children. So we just stored up our belongings, packed up what we needed and took off! Oh, to be that young again! This time, it was not the James Cagle family who decided the move. The United States Army decided to change their minds about the guarantee about no overseas work, but they gave everyone the opportunity to take an honorable discharge if they so desired, and so we did. And we once again faced the unemployment line back in Lauderdale County. James has always been very resourceful so I never worried about his being out of work for long. This time, he went to work for Reynolds. He bought some property in the Moody Hollow and built a house, part of which is now still standing as "Aunt Cat and Uncle Junior's House". I survived there, but I was never happy there because James had to work such long hours, and I was afraid there after dark with my children. I was also afraid of my old cows. They didn't like me, and I didn't like them! I truly knew I was not a country girl. I wanted nothing to do with milking! When I tried to milk, the old striped cow (brindled) I think they called it, would lower her head and run me. I could out run her, but I got the best end of the deal. She didn't get milked! But James was irritated with me. He was on the 4 to 12 shift. It was not his fault that I had to do the milking, or that I had to hear the screech owls, or that I imagined every wolf in the county was coming after me! There were no houses anywhere around! I couldn't let my children know how scared I was. I was not frightened of people, which I should have been, but of the unknown. Our house had a tin roof, and it made all sorts of weird noises.

It was at the end of this year that we were at our lowest ebb financially. James had been laid off and was drawing $20 a week unemployment. We had two beautiful little girls and nothing to buy Santa for them. Grandaddy Cagle found out about our situation (I don't know who told him.), and he loaned us $20. We bought our girls a little red wagon and a baby doll each. They were so happy.

I know the reader probably wonders why there is no more written about my Johnson family than there is at this time. It was during this time that the direction of our lives seemed to change. We, Sister and I, still saw each other on a regular basis, but somehow we did not have as much in common as we did before we were married. Perhaps because we both tended to favor our in-laws as much as possible, and they were very different from each other. We tended to drift slowly apart. We were both trying desperately to hold on to our marriages and to make happy home lives for our families. We were still deeply committed to each other, however, and were still very much committed to our Johnson family. Our brothers were busy making lives of their own, and Mother was so busy with Mr. Alexander, going on the insurance route with him everyday, still teaching music at home and at Anderson school, and looking after the tenant farmers on the farm. My life seemed to take a different path after my marriage. I no longer lived with my mother, nor did I attend the Baptist church of which I had been a faithful member all my life. This change did not happen abruptly, but seemed to be a natural progression, taking place over a number of years. I was now a member of the church of Christ. I was baptized into the church in 1947, the year Cathy was born. I had been hesitant about changing my religious affiliation for a number of years, but I decided to do so on this particular summer, at this particular time, when James was away. I was baptized in Mince Creek down below our little dream house. I remember wearing Granddaddy Cagle's overcoat with a pin to hold it down. Brother Edwards, from Texas, was the visiting preacher who baptized me. I now felt that all my questions about my faith in God had been answered, and that I truly wanted to worship Him in spirit and in truth. Whatever doubts or fears I had had were all laid to rest, and I was now at peace once again. I was now a truly changed Johnson, but one who would always love her Johnson family as well as her newly adopted Cagle family.

The decade from 1945 to 1955 was filled with turbulence as well as calmness, joy as well as sorrow, and unforgettable events which would shape our lives forever. From the birth of Carolyn in 1945 to the death of Mother in 1955 stretched a period of seemingly endless joy and sorrow. In this short period of ten years, we filled our lives with so many unforgettable events.

Marilyn

After little Carolyn and Cathy had their Christmas in the "Moody Hollow" with their little red wagons, we moved to an apartment on Tombigbee Street in Florence, in the same home as Willie T and E.F. There Willie T and I awaited together the births of our new little babies—Willie T and E.F. were expecting Franky and James and I awaited Marilyn. James was working with T.V.A., and it was more convenient to live close to Dr. Rhea, who was in Sheffield, and guess what? For the first time I got to tell a doctor I was pregnant, have an exam before the birth, and actually have a so-called "due date." However, Marilyn did not come on that due date. I was tired and wanted to have my baby; so we sent Carolyn and Cathy to Mama Cagle's and I proceeded to walk—literally pace—back and forth. Dr. Rhea suggested that I take Castor oil if I wanted my baby to come early; so I did, and so she did! A beautiful black-haired baby girl was born at ECM hospital. The nurses put a pink bow ribbon in her hair when she was shown to me 2 days after her birth! I had some problems during the birth process, had to have my tubes tied, and required additional blood, but everything worked out well. Buddy and E.F. both offered to give blood to me, but neither could afford to lose any of their own. Since I was negative, as Mother was, a friend very graciously donated his blood for me, and I rallied very quickly and was anxious to get started with my new little family. Now, at the age of 21 I had my perfect little family—3 lovely daughters. God had been so gracious to me! Mother once again came to my rescue and cared for my little one. Marilyn was such a good baby, and Carolyn and Cathy welcomed her with open arms--too open at times! I think she must have been born with her thumb in her mouth. As she grew older, I would find her asleep with her pillow and her thumb in a corner under the ironing board or on the couch.

After a few short months we moved back to New Georgia. This time just up the hill from New Georgia

Cathy, Carolyn, Marilyn

church. Marilyn was only three or four months old, and I enjoyed strolling her in the buggy down to Mother's house (which later became our home). Cathy and Carolyn loved the walk also even though their little legs grew tired before we got there. I usually had the buggy filled with laundry as well as the baby since our well was always low of water. I remember on one occasion at this home I suddenly felt overwhelmed. I was nursing Marilyn and reading to Carolyn and Cathy, who were also sitting on my lap. They were two and four years old and they all three went to sleep!! I couldn't move. I panicked! The book fell from my lap, and I suddenly wondered just what I had done with my life! I was 22 years old and was literally and figuratively tied down! Then I looked down in my arms at those beautiful little girls. One with golden locks and two with dark tresses, all three holding me tightly as I rocked back and forth. I think it was at that moment in time that I knew how much God had blessed me with these little girls and how fortunate James and I were to have each other and to be the parents of Carolyn, Cathy, and Marilyn Cagle. From that moment on, I have never regretted our impetuous moves and unusual undertakings because we have always had our entire family in consideration. I will have to say, though, that perhaps I shouldn't have tried feeding my baby adult food quite as early as I did! Pinto beans at three months? Even mashed up, that's a bit risky, I believe! I chalk that up to youth and inexperience. Back to moves, TVA once again transferred James. This time to Pickwick Dam in Savannah, Tennessee. So once again, we packed up our babies and away we went. We truly enjoyed our short stay in Savannah. The girls enjoyed playing on the playgrounds nearby, and we enjoyed playing tennis when James got home from work. However, this job didn't last long, and James decided to go back into the car business.

This time we moved back to Florence on Houston Street where we enrolled our precious little Carolyn Jean into first grade at Gilbert School where Little Ralph had enrolled a year earlier but was now in Detroit. Carolyn felt so big. She could walk to school, and Mrs. Reeder was her teacher. Mother was so proud of my girls. She made them matching navy suits and white blouses and taught them to sing "Mammy's Little Baby Loves Shortning Bread" when Marilyn was only 2 ½ years old. She also insisted that the girls take piano lessons from her even when they were so young they couldn't read the notes. They were in Mother's recitals from the time they were 3 or 4 years old.

By this time, car business was truly James' forte. He seemed to live and

Carolyn, Cathy, Marilyn

breathe the business. We needed to move so we could be closer to his work; so we moved to Dover Avenue in Sheffield where our little girls once again enrolled in a new school. This was old business for Carolyn by now. Cathy was a bit more shy, and Marilyn was not old enough to attend, but they were all old enough to get "red" measles which Cathy brought home to the family. One by one the girls got that disease along with chicken pox for added measure. The poor babies were so very ill. We were so fortunate to have Billy Ray and Shirley Cagle, James' baby brother and sister, to help us out during these trying times. Mother was still in Detroit and so were Sister and Robert. It was about this time that I started thinking about returning to school for my senior high credits. I only lacked one semester each in English and history, and I didn't think it would be so hard to complete that much. Mother was very enthusiastic about the idea, but we just left it at that stage—and I continued reading everything I could get my hands on. But I had always been an avid reader so this was not hard to do.

Carolyn, Cathy, Marilyn

Just as my Johnson family seemed to be making moves to come back home, James and I decided to move to Mississippi to go into car business with Randall and JoAnn Goggins, close friends of ours who had a Pontiac dealership in Pontotoc, Mississippi. Mother was coming home from Detroit to move to Sheffield. Sister was getting a job at Penney's, and my little brother was getting married, but all this will be described in another chapter of this book. This section's focus is on our experiences in Mississippi. And what experiences they were! First of all, we found a wonderful little church in which to worship with a dynamic young preacher named Clifford Payne. Next, we grew to truly care for Randall and JoAnne and their adorable little girl, Suzanne.

We were excited about being on our own once again—all five of us in a brand new state. We had never lived in Mississippi before. We felt so independent! (for at least a month!) Then we started to get just a little homesick. It was too far to go back to New Georgia to worship each Sunday, but it was too near to act as though we had moved so far away! Well, we sort of met this thing half way. We drove home about once a month (maybe twice), and the rest of the time enjoyed our Lord's day worshipping at Pontotoc church of Christ. Our little girls were happy wherever we were so we kept the road busy and the wheels rolling. I don't think we were missed at New Georgia too much! My Johnson family didn't miss me since they were all way up north in Detroit exploring the other side of the USA.

At this time our little Carolyn was so accustomed to changing schools, nothing seemed to daunt her. Cathy, on the other hand, was much more shy and reserved. We didn't realize until much later the psychological impact the change of schools would have on our children. Marilyn would just pull her pillow up a little tighter and hide her thumb, which was in her mouth. Carolyn straightened up her shoulders and strutted out her chin in a belligerent manner, but Cathy ran away at every opportunity. However, once the girls were all corralled in one place, it was amazing what they could accomplish. They could belt out "Mammie's Little Baby" and smile at the audience as though they were the happiest little girls in the USA. My heart aches when I think about the times I should have been holding them close in my arms instead of pushing them up on the stage. But they continued to win awards in Mississippi just as they did in Alabama (see picture).

After about a year in Pontotoc, James was offered 51 percent of a Studebaker dealership in Houston, Mississippi, which is about 25 miles south of Pontotoc. What an exciting opportunity! Houston is a farming community, and we were welcomed there with open arms. We rented a sweet little home with quite a bit of acreage outside the city and the girls truly enjoyed playing on the grounds which included a couple of fish ponds. Their Uncle Bill came and visited with them and taught them to fish. It was while we were living there that Cathy started to the first grade and decided school was not her forte, so she quit. We had to go find her!

Cathy, Marilyn & Carolyn.

When I think back now about my own childhood insecurities, I can see why Cathy decided running was an option, but at the time I only thought she was homesick for Alabama, which of course, was partially true. Cathy remembers an incident in school in which one student misbehaved so the teacher punished the entire class. This method of punishment remained in Cathy's memory as a blurb for the rest of her young life. Another bad memory she had of Mississippi (of me incidentally) was an

Marilyn

occasion at school when she dropped her crayons, and I refused to pick them up for her! I don't remember that incident, but mothers should be so careful about the feelings of their children. It is so important to let them know how much you care for them. While you want to teach them independence, it should not come at the price of your showing your deep love for your children. I think I was still learning how to be a mother. I had had no courses, I had started out so young, but these are not excuses. My children were and still are the most important people in the world to me. Now, before I digress, where was I? Oh yes, in the 1st grade classroom with Cathy. Well, now, lets move over to the 3rd grade classroom where Carolyn so desperately wanted the leading role of Madame Butterfly in the little school operatta. There seemed to be a vendetta going on in the classroom. All the little girls were saying, "let's vote for so and so" who had been there longer of course than Carolyn. So Carolyn didn't get the lead.

Instead, she got the role of the narrator, which of course, was more important, for it had a much longer narration. But to Carolyn, only Madame Butterfly was "the role", so she cried bitterly. Well, all things didn't go bright and cheerful in Houston, did they? But the play was a success, Carolyn read her part beautifully, the girls sang in the program. Marilyn looked like a living doll, and you would never have known that Cathy had to pick up her own crayons. James seemed unaware of all the drama taking place in our home lives since he was busy trying to establish a successful Studebaker agency in Houston. He had a nice building with an attractive showroom and a beautiful secretary of whom I was just a little jealous, especially since Marilyn seemed to like her so well. Seriously, I had too much time on my hands. My children were in school, my husband was working, so I needed something to do also. I was not so happy either. By this time, my family was migrating back from up north, and I wanted to be a part of them again. I was also having some

physical problems which were hard to combat at this time. I was continuing to study for my last semester in high school (which I never made) so I read Shakespeare, Dante, Shelly, and Keats, at every opportunity I had. I also read the history of

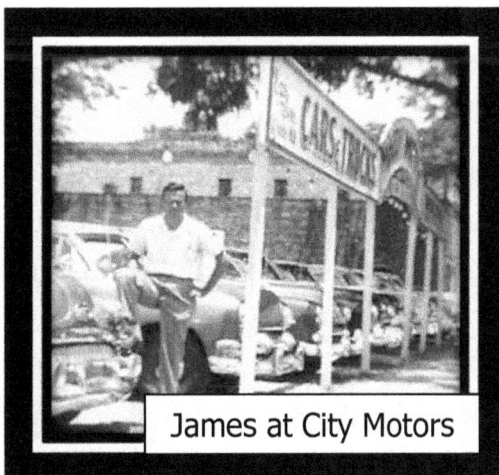

James at City Motors

Alabama and everything else I thought might help me when I entered into twelfth grade after so many years out of school.

But there were Cagle's to the rescue! It was while we were in Houston that E.F. and Willie T decided to move down and be with us for awhile. What an adventure that was! It broke the monotony of the long winter months and the hot summer months. They had two little boys, Franky, Marilyn's age, and a darling little baby, Andy, whom the girls adored (and still do). Having the E.F. Cagle Family with us seemed to make Houston more like home. It was also in Houston that we first met Brother Lindsey Allen, who later became such a dear friend of our family. At this time, we were worshipping with the Houston church of Christ. Brother Lindsey Allen was the preacher there. Brother Allen was a visiting preacher who stayed with us in Mississippi as well as later in Alabama.

Car business is slow in a farming city. James grew anxious as months passed and business continued to be slow. Economy was slow nation-wide, but we had a little family to provide for and farmers were not too interested in shopping for new cars. After many thoughtful months filled with figures, plans, and prayers, we decided our best bet was to sell our share of the business and move back to Tuscumbia, Alabama, were James was offered a job with City Motors, a DeSoto/Plymouth dealership in Florence. We were quite close to the Sheffield library so I checked out books on High School Equivalency Examinations, which I had heard of but didn't know anything about. There were summaries of all academics—take your choice—so I took them all, studied them while my children were in school. We enrolled Marilyn in Mrs. Vess's kindergarten in Tuscumbia, which was just at the end of the street where we lived (206 Almon Avenue) across from the Helen Keller Home in Tuscumbia. Our home was not too far from Mother's house on Montgomery Avenue in Sheffield so I was so fortunate to get to see her so often. Little did I know what she had in mind for me! In the mean-time, our sweet little girls were once more enrolled in a new school! This time Cave Street Elementary in Tuscumbia where they walked to school each day. Cathy says she still does not remember anything about these school years. They must have been so traumatic for her! May God forgive us for putting our children through all these changes. We truly loved them all this time, but we didn't realize what these moves could do to sensitive little minds! While in Tuscumbia, we attended Fourth Street church of Christ. Mother was across town at South-Side Baptist.

One day I came home and found out Mother had called UNA, which was Florence State Teachers College at that time, and asked about the qualifications necessary for one to take the GED which had been announced in the newspaper. Earlier we had contacted Lauderdale County High about taking the last semester of high school, and Mr. Clay, the principal, said the GED test was available for some, and it would be much better for me if I could take it. So I signed up for the test and took it, which involved English, history, social science, science, and math. I made the highest scores in English and math, but I passed them all so I could have majored in any of them. Dr. McElheny suggested that I major in English, and he was anxious for me to enroll immediately at UNA. I couldn't believe what was happening. I had never received my diploma from high school, but I was about to enroll in college! My darling mother and my darling husband had promised each other that I would continue my education, so I did—and so I am—until this very day!

The James Cagle Family

Chapter 21: Lucille 1946-1953

1946 was a very busy year for the Ralph Wilson family. Ralph was still driving a truck and had to be away from us more than he wanted to be. I never had a dull moment, so much was going on with two little boys only thirteen months apart. Ralph J. really loved his little brother and enjoyed entertaining him. I had to tie Denny in the high chair so Ralph could not pull him out. I was so fortunate that Denny was such a good baby. Little Ralph was learning to walk, run, talk and potty all in this year. I spent so many happy hours pushing them in a buggy to our city park which was only a block away. I would let them play in the pretty grass there. I took a blanket, spread it on the ground and enjoyed the nice, peaceful quiet park across from the post office.

Louise Tuberville would bring Jimmy Joe and Willa Jean would come down and bring Carolyn Jean for a fun filled day in the park. Even though the apartment was very inconvenient because of the many stairs, I enjoyed our time on Mobile Street for all the nice sidewalks to push buggies and later to push strollers and pull wagons on. In the middle of 1946, we moved to Prospect Street to a comfortable, ground level apartment that mother owned. Denny was walking and really getting around. He and Ralph J. always played together so well. I really enjoyed my babies so much. I read to them and played with them while they were awake. I did my laundry and house work while they took their naps. We attended Central Baptist Church very faithfully never missing anything unless we were sick. I worked in the nursery and toddler department in Sunday school and helped with the music when needed.

Through these busy years Ralph was an "on the road" truck driver for Baggett Transportation Company. This kept him away from home so many days, but he really enjoyed his time with us when he was home. Because of the rough times that he had never been exposed to before, due to his sheltered home life, he became overwhelmed by the excitement of the results of alcohol. His life spiraled out of control and resulted in a severe stomach problem.

Ralph's emotional and physical problem affected the entire family. When Ralph had to give up his trucking job, we moved into a doll-like house, converted chicken house, which Ralph had remodeled in his parent's backyard at 125Royal Avenue. The boys were thrilled to be so close to Mammaw and Granddaddy along with Sis, Lee, and Glenn who were still at home. What a Wilson family--Ruth, Pearson and Dale Blackburn, Grace, Vernon, Grace and Karen Stutts, Elden, Doris, and

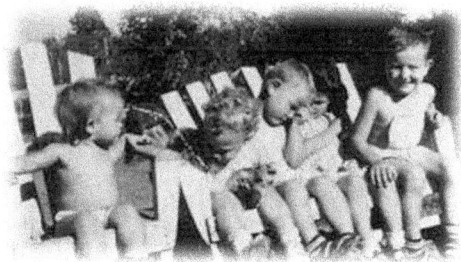

Cathy, Janet, Denny, Carolyn & Ralph

Jimmy Wilson. Coming by on weekends for all the family was fun, food, and fellowship. It gave my boys something to always remember about their Wilson family—all going to Central Baptist Church, which was only a few blocks away.

While Ralph loved being with his family, his weakness for alcohol still had to be dealt with. Local doctors recommended treatment at the VA Hospital in

Memphis. Ralph spent several months at the hospital there. The boys and I took advantage of our visits there to see him to go to the Memphis zoo.

Life went on and we visited mother frequently, enjoying our visits. Ralph J. and Denny loved to play with their first cousins Janet, Carolyn Jean, and Cathy who lived nearby.

During the time that Ralph was away, I had to provide for my family. I cleaned a few homes in my neighborhood for $1.00 each. I always took my two little boys with me. They sat on the couch in the living room with their books to look at. I would start in the kitchen and work my way through the house. I also made extra money by taking in ironing, after Mr. Wilson bought me a new iron. As you can see, I was learning new trades. I was determined not to leave my sons, until they were older, to work outside our home.

During these hard times, all of our relatives were so good to us. Mother and Mr. Alex made frequent visits, always leaving goodies for the children and vegetables from the farm for us. Mr. Wilson, very quietly, left a ten dollar bill on our table every Friday. He expected no "pat on the back," but he always knew how much it was appreciated.

Because Ralph was a veteran and away in the VA hospital, my boys and I were invited to the First Methodist Church in downtown Florence to a Christmas party where Santa Claus would greet the children with gifts. The party was to start at 6 p.m., it was bitterly cold, the walk would be about ten blocks. I bundled the boys up on their warmest outerwear, beautiful little navy overcoats, made from Uncle Glenn's Navy uniform. I carried Denny in my left arm and led Ralph J. with my right hand, stopping every few blocks to switch arms. The boys were so good.

When we arrived, I looked over the crowd and immediately decided we did not belong there. The boys did not understand when I said we were going home. Ralph J. questioned why we were not staying to see Santa. I loved him, gave him a big hug and told him that we would see Santa somewhere else. We walked back down Mobile Street to our little home. It was very cold, but we played a game on our way. The street lights were pretty and bright so we could watch our steps. We walked, we ran, we hopped, and tried to skip to take our disappointment away.

Later that same week, Mother came for a visit. She took me to a hardware store, across the street from the post office where I bought two little red metal chairs which I still have, and now my great-grandchildren sit in. (Now you know why they are so precious to me.) We had a wonderful Christmas because Ralph was able to come home. No money could buy the love we four shared.

Following Ralph's release from the VA hospital, we continued to live at 126 Royal Avenue where the boys grew physically, emotionally, intellectually, and spiritually. We were very active at church, still attending Central Baptist. We have so many happy memories of those times. Denny always wanted to be like his big brother. The year Ralph was given a certificate of promotion to the Beginner Department in Sunday school, big tears rolled down Denny's cheeks because he did not receive one just like his brother. Mrs. Edgar Johnson, the department leader, saw those big tears and immediately took a small paper and wrote, "Denny you are such a sweet little boy", and gave it to him. How his brown eyes sparkled, and the tears were gone replaced by a happy smile. He thought it was a certificate of promotion.

Kindergarten opened up a whole new world for us. When Ralph J. was five years old, he started his schooling at Maud Lindsey Kindergarten near Brandon School. On the first day he came home all excited and told us he had a friend whose name was Wilson also. He and Myron Wilson have remained very good friends through all these years. A year later when Denny attended the same kindergarten, he came home saying, "I have a sweetheart, and her name is Sue." Sue Watkins and Denny graduated from Coffee High School together and are still friends today.

Meanwhile our home lives were changing also. Ralph had a full time job, a taxi driver. We moved to North Florence to be closer to his work and the children's school. Oh, how we hated to leave our tiny, sweet little house on Royal Avenue, but this move proved to be very smart, because it gave us the chance to send our boys to Gilbert School which was such an outstanding educational facility. It was the foundation for all their educational endeavors.

Once we moved to North Florence, we stayed in that part of town. We lived across the street from Highland Baptist on Chisholm Road for several years. Ralph J.'s first six weeks of school was at Patton Elementary because we were still on Royal Avenue. His teacher Mrs. Acker thought he was so pretty and sweet, she kept him on her lap most of the time; but oh, what a difference when he transferred to Gilbert School. His first grade teacher was Mrs. Mauvine Reeder. What a great teacher, every little boy should have a "Mrs. Reeder" for first grade because she taught independence and self-confidence. Denny and I walked Ralph to school and went back to walk him home each day for six weeks; then Mrs. Reeder said, "He does not need you little Mother." After that he was on his own—my little boy was growing up, and by this time Denny was asking, "Mother can I go by myself?" Denny was always independent! One example of his independence was the time he stopped at Chatterbox restaurant on Wood Avenue and climbed very nonchalantly on a bar stool and requested a cup of coffee, laying a dine on the counter, remember he was only six years old! The waitress asked if his parents allowed him to drink coffee. His reply was, "Yes, but we were out of coffee, and I'm afraid I'll have a headache without the coffee." Denny knew how to speak with authority even at a young age.

We really enjoyed living on Chisholm Road. Our house was only one block from Seven Points in North Florence. The Bevis Family lived next door to us. The children were Shirley, Jim, and Billy. All such wonderful playmates for our sons. Their father, Pete, was in the army.

Ralph & his taxi

Denny, Rip & Ralph J

160

So a single (for a while) mom was next door and a super friend to me. Clara was a nurse at ECM. We helped each other so much by caring for each other's children. While living there, the boys had a pretty dog named Rip. One cold, snowy weekend, he just disappeared. We tried to find him, but no luck. Snow fell all weekend, and we were so worried, but the next week, we heard a scratching sound at our front door, and guess who was there—"Rip". He was so clean and dry. Someone must have had him in out of the cold. He was so happy and so were we.

Ralph loved to take the boys and me to Cyprus Creek to fish and just walk around the banks of the creek. He decided to build a little boat (canoe type) for fun. He spent many afternoons building it, and when it was finished, he let Ralph and Denny help paint it green. Then down to the water we went, of course Rip was included in this big adventure--the launching of this little boat. Ralph put both the boys in the boat along with Rip. Of course, he waded out in the shallow water with the boys and the boat. They were having a great time, and guess what? Water started slowly filing the bottom of the boat, and boys, boat, and Rip started easing down. Ralph helped them out, and they enjoyed playing in the water a while. So much for boat building!

Ralph's problem had reoccurred so, he was admitted to the VA hospital leaving the boys and me trying to decide on our next move—sweet brother Buddy to the rescue. At that time he was employed as teacher/coach at Saint Michael Catholic School in Saint Florian, the only Protestant teacher in that private school. He and Jo opened their heart and home to us. Our household possessions were stored at Mother's house, and the boys and I moved to Buddy and Jo's home. He forgot that we had about 8 or 9 little chickens that the boys had received for Easter—so Bud made a little make-shift chicken pen. Ralph was dismissed from the hospital after 3 weeks. His uncle Dewey Coker had come to the Wilson's for a visit, so Ralph brought him to Bud's and was ready to take us home. Ralph had rented a house on Indiana Street in North Florence for us. As we packed up and prepared to move again, Bud got me aside and said, "Sister, you and the boys are always welcome, but the damn chickens have got to go" (the only time I had ever heard my precious brother curse)!

Mother in Detroit at her music studio

In anticipation of a career in teaching piano, Mother took several courses in advanced teaching techniques and advanced studies at Wayne University in Detroit. After she moved back to Alabama, she took a home study course from Wayne University called "Teaching Piano". I have really learned so much from that material which helped me to prepare for teaching piano. She was so happy to live close to that wonderful school and took advantage of going there many times. (See

Lucille and boys at the studio

picture of Mother outside her music studio.)

Other events were happening in our family that would shape our lives forever. We were already contemplating a move to Detroit. Mother and Mr. Alex were already in Detroit where Mother had rented a building in preparation for a Music Studio which she planned to open later. Mr. Alex was employed by Chrysler Manufacturing Company. Our little brother Robert (6'2") had just recently married Mildred Kretzer (May 15, 1950) and was also living there. Denny and Ralph were thrilled with the prospect of living with Mammy and Pop as well as expecting to see snow in the northern state.

After getting unpacked and settled, next order of business was getting our boys enrolled in school, which in this case was just across the street from Mammy's studio— our living quarters were in the back. Denny and Ralph, who were so accustomed to being accepted as they were, were shocked when they were told they would not be in the grades they had expected to be in. We were told by the principal that all parents of children from Alabama, Tennessee, Mississippi, and Georgia should line up on the left side of the room. These parents were told that because of the educational system in the south, their children would be demoted one grade level. I was furious!! I was the only parent who refused to accept that ultimatum. I showed my children's grade reports, and I firmly requested permission for them to be placed in first and

Ralph J., Lucille, Denny

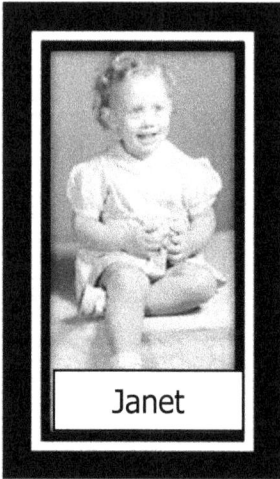

second grades. They reluctantly agreed. After six weeks the boys' perfect grades proved their Mother was correct.

So now, guess what? When the first real snow arrived in Detroit, the Wilson's departed. Ralph had a job at Kroger Warehouse, but it was not in North Florence, and he had just bought a little old car, I don't know the kind or brand, but it looked round on both ends, and there was room for the boys to cuddle up in the back. There they could watch the snow slowly receding in the background—at least they did see snow. Mother hated to see us leave, but she understood the importance of family.

Janet

Janie

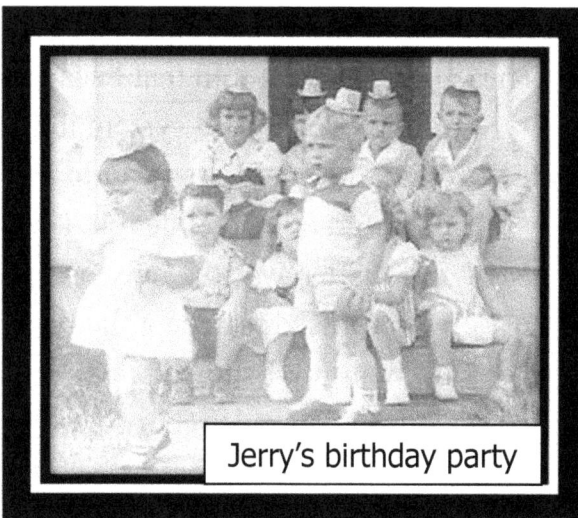

Jerry's birthday party

On our arrival in Florence, Buddy and Jo opened their home to us. We really enjoyed our stay with them on Calhoun Drive. Buddy had left the teaching position and was working as a supervisor for Reynolds Aluminum Company, a large plant in Sheffield. This gave him better pay and benefits. Jo was working as a hairstylist at Mary Snow's beauty shop in East Florence. They were now blessed with three lovely children—Janet 6, Jerry 4, and Janie who was still a cuddly little one. Our children were so happy to have cousins to play with. Ralph and I both went job hunting the very first week we were back in Florence and were both fortunate in finding employment at once. The boys were enrolled in their former school, Gilbert, with the same playmates, and life was back to normal.

Little did I know what the future would hold for me with the J.C. Penney Company for the next fifty-one years. They were great years, filled with lasting friendships and a secure livelihood.

Somehow I must have known that J.C. Penney was in my future. I started out in the morning when the stores first opened on Court Street, putting in applications at each store except Rogers because I knew I could not dress according to their dress code (since I had on clothes borrowed from Willa Jean and Jo.) Little did I dream that within a year, I

Lucille at Penny's | Ralph, Lucille & City Cab Co.

165

would be the dress buyer at J.C.P. When I stopped at Wilson's Fabric store, Mr. Ellis Wilson, the owner, begged me to come back in about an hour when his wife would be there because he really wanted two Lucille Wilson's working for him (his wife was named Lucille), but on down the street to J.C. Penney I went. I met the manager at Penney's who escorted me to the personnel office where I filled out an application which he immediately reviewed, and I was hired on the spot. I started the next day working in Ladies Sportswear and Ready-to-Wear. What a job! And just think—I made .60 per hour, but after all, that was much better than the one dollar a day for ironing, so I was coming up in the world. Seriously, I could go to work now on a daily basis, knowing that Ralph's job as taxi driver for North Florence Cab Company would allow him to pick up the boys and care for them until I was home from Penney's.

Now that we both had jobs, we found a home on Button Avenue in North Florence which seemed to just fit our family. It was a split level (not fancy, just on a sloping lot) just perfect for two boys to entertain their neighborhood friends. David Hollis lived next door, Lewis and Wendell Olive were close by. There was also room for my piano, which meant I could now begin teaching piano lessons— something I had longed to do for many years!

At this time I began my three career life— homemaker, mother and wife, J.C. Penney Company, and music teacher—and oh, how my sons dreaded the yearly music recitals, but they always participated in them, both mine and Mother's recitals. By this time Mother had missed her family so much she had also packed her bags and returned home and settled down on Montgomery

Avenue in Sheffield, Alabama, where she immediately continued teaching music. Mr. Alex continued his profession as a salesman, this time as a self-employed owner and salesman of used cars.

Robert and Mildred followed Mother back south and bought a cozy little home in Muscle Shoals. This is where they started their family—where Jonathan was born. During all this time when the Alexanders, Wilson and Johnson families were exploring the wilds of the north, Willa Jean and James had taken their three little girls and headed toward the south, toward Pontotoc and Houston, Mississippi, where they bought a Studebaker car agency. Willa Jean will be telling all about her adventures in her preceding chapter.

Mother, always believing that you do a better job of serving the Lord when you go to the nearest church of your faith, joined Southside Baptist church. She became a wonderful, faithful member, serving as pianist for the church and later as pianist for the Colbert, Lauderdale Baptist Association.

The early 1950's were happy days for the Ralph Wilson family—both boys were so happy in school making good grades and having so many good friends at Gilbert school—they loved the entire faculty including the principal Mr. Grady Richards, 1st grade Mrs. Mauvine Reader, 2nd grade Ms. Little, 3rd grade Miss Verta Jones, 4th grade Ms. Shoemaker and Ms. Pittman. In the early 50's, the teachers had an opportunity to choose their next year's students at the end of the school year, helping to fill the classes as much as possible. Denny was always chosen to follow Ralph. My sons are so different it was not a surprise that the teachers could not help but show a little favoritism at times. Mrs. Little, second grade teacher, loved Ralph so much and shared with me an incident she would remember forever. Ralph had a paper bag, he blew it up and "popped" it. He had a look of fright and horror, so shocked that he had made such a noise and it was very disturbing in class, but Mrs. Little was still more shocked. Could that be Ralph Wilson, her wonderful, favorite student? The third grade teacher Miss Verta Jones made no secret that Denny was a #1 favorite of hers. She told me, "Denny is a little man in a class of young children." The boys never felt jealous of each other and it never seemed to bother them. In later years we decided to send Denny to the University of Alabama in Tuscaloosa, a school where no one knew he had an older brother named Ralph. When they were in the 5th and 6th grades, they were transferred to Harlan School for one year. It was a new school and North Florence students were rezoned for a while. Mr. Young was another wonderful principal. The teachers were very good also. These years were very busy for me. I was very involved with PTA (a vice-president one year) and every week, I would go from JC Penney to Gilbert schools each Wednesday afternoon and help all classes with music. I also was very involved with the boys in cub scouts. Before 7 a.m. each morning the boys wanted to get to school to play ball with their special friend "Bugs" Dunn, who lived down the street . Another super friend was Robert Potts, who later became president of UNA.

All the while I was busy at J.C. Penney Company, being promoted to department manager (the first female in that position in Alabama) taking on all buying for the children's department and the toy department. I was so blessed having a wonderful manager, Mr. Ed Skelton, who encouraged me and helped me so much in all my promotions in the company. He and his lovely wife Bettie were great friends to me. One example, they never missed one of my music recitals – that was real friendship. My daily schedule at work required finding good help to take care of my sons in the after school hours and on Saturday. We tried several different people, but had no real success. We finally decided that Ralph would pick them up at school and take them to Mother's house, and she was always happy to see them. Aunt Grace Stutts was also called upon sometimes, she lived on Chisholm Road in Florence. Ralph D's taxi job was perfect during these years, taking the boys to little league, after school activities, etc. He also took me to and from J.C. Penney's. Our store hours were from 9 to 5:30 each day except Wednesday. We closed at noon on Wednesday. In later years, we started staying open until 9 on Fridays - no Sunday work.

Ralph D. was also enjoying his job as a taxi driver. He made so many lasting friends that he made regular trips to and from work with, Mrs. Harris, private secretary to the manager of Sears, and other regular customers who helped him decide that he should have his own taxi company. So, he did just that. He started his own service in about 1953. We moved up the street on Button

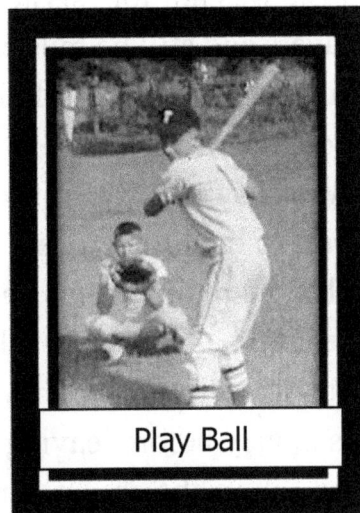

Play Ball

Avenue to a small house, but with a huge yard, plenty of room for a ball field in the back, also perfect for camping out under a tent during summer nights. This was our first house to own. We bought it from a Mr. Taylor.

The most important factor in our family life was deep faith in God. We were always thankful for all our blessings He gave us. We attended Central Baptist Church through these many years, never considering changing to a church in North Florence because so many of our Wilson family were there. I sang in the choir, taught Sunday school, worked in church training, and helped in any way I could. Ralph and Denny accepted Christ as Savior and were baptized at Central Baptist when they were eight and nine years old. I'll never forget some advice Mother gave me when they would drag their feet getting ready for Wednesday night, she said, "Sister, you don't ask if they are going to school, you ask, what are you going to wear today, do the same about church."

Mother started Ralph and Denny in music at this time, encouraging them to practice and teaching them that music was not for "sissies". They could be great ball players and still be musicians. They really loved all the time they spent with Mother and they still reminiscence about the many things she taught them. Denny always loved spaghetti, and one day Mother sent him down the street to the little grocery store to get him a can of spaghetti. When he returned and started to give Mother the change, she asked, "Is it correct change?" After checking it, he said, "No, it is short one penny." She told him to always count his money before leaving and suggested that he take it all back, show the grocery man the mistake, and get his penny—which he gladly did. A good lesson in financial affairs.

Ralph J and Denny both loved to play ball. They started little league when they were eight and nine years old. Ralph played with the Red Socks, Denny played with the Tigers. Oh, how they loved it. We spent many hours at McFarland Ball Field watching every game. In the fall, football took over. They started playing, but because of asthma, Ralph J. had to give it up. Denny played several years and enjoyed it.

Chapter 22: 1954-1955 Willa Jean and Lucille

What a memorable 4th of July! We all met at Mother's on Montgomery Avenue for the day. Mother was not feeling up to par, but she did not want anyone to notice. Janie and Johnny were toddlers. Ralph, Denny and Jerry were outside playing ball; the girls, Carolyn, Janet, Cathy, and Marilyn were inside playing school or dolls. All we adults were jabbering and

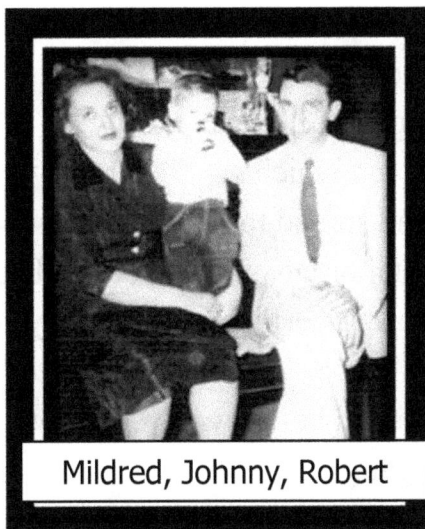

Mildred, Johnny, Robert

visiting. Mother, our strong one in the family, suddenly showed signs of weakness, fainting away. After she was

Janie & Johnny

revived, she tried to play down any problem she had, blaming it all on the hot weather. After all, she had never had to go to the doctor. We children, especially Robert, insisted that she see Dr. Muhlendorf, a friend of the family, right away.

The next day, Mother, accompanied by all four of her children, met Dr. Muhlendorf at the Colbert County Hospital where he explained that he would prefer her having emergency surgery which should only take about an hour. Four hours later he came out from surgery to tell us that she had incurable cancer of the colon which had spread to many

Mother at her beloved piano

vital organs in her body. He suggested the only thing to do was to perform a colostomy at once, leaving all vital organs in place. After we agreed to this procedure, many hours passed before we were allowed to see our dear Mother again.

When Mother revived, however, she did not seem discouraged. On the other hand, she tried to build up our spirits. She was smiling and cheerful and she remembered right away that tomorrow night was Wednesday night, and she was supposed to play the piano for Southside Baptist

Mr. Alex & Mother, 1954

Church. She asked for Mary Ann Byers, who was about twelve years old at the time and one of Mother's most advanced piano students. After Mary Ann came to the hospital, Mother gave her a very encouraging talk assuring her that she could play several hymns all in the key of C or G for Wednesday night church service and to get with Gary Menne and help choose about four hymns until Mother was well enough to return.

We were advised before Mother left the hospital that Mother would only have a short time to live. We were all in a state of shock. Our Mother had always been the healthy one in the family, a believer in herbs, lotions, and medicinal cures. She seldom called on doctors and never had gone to a hospital before this surgery. We decided together that we would not discuss Mother's illness with her. After all, she was going to beat this illness. She always did!

Mother continued teaching music from her home on Montgomery Avenue in Sheffield after she returned from the hospital in July. Her first recital was in the Fall of the same year (see picture). While Mother was busy with her music, we children tried to act as normal as possible, carrying on our own lives, outwardly normal, but inwardly suffering

excruciating pain, knowing that we were losing our mother and that we could do nothing about it. Buddy worked as supervisor at Reynolds Metals - a job he assumed after leaving the teaching profession; Lucille, management at J.C. Penny Company; Willa Jean, enrolled at Florence State Teachers College in the field of education, and Robert as salesman at Southern Sash in Sheffield and West Monroe, Louisiana. We were all surrounding Mother, but could do nothing to ease her physical pain (of which she refused to acknowledge anyway). By this time, she was slowly losing weight, but becoming more beautiful every day.

Cathy, Carolyn & Marilyn in dresses made by Mammy for her last recital.

Chapter 23: Thoughts by Lucille 1954-1955

1954 was a banner year for our family yet the saddest news I had ever had was in July 1954. My job at J.C. Penney was growing each year—promotions and much more responsibility. I welcomed it because it meant an increase in pay. Mother was so proud of my job. She would come in the store to my hat department, sit down, and try on pretty hats; she still loved to dress up. I remember her last visit to the store with me. She looked tired, but I thought it was the hot weather.

My life, and that of our entire family, took a drastic change after Mother's surgery in July 1954. I wanted to be with her all the time I could, yet my job and family was demanding more from me. When Willa Jean and I received the sad news that Mother's days were limited, we went to Willa Jean's house, fell across a bed together and cried for hours. How could we go on? Yet, we had to. We had to make some plans of who could do what? We needed to take care of Mother. I caught a bus in Florence, rode to Sheffield, got off on Montgomery Avenue, and walked to Mother and Mr. Alex's home, changed her bed, helped clean the house, and helped Willa Jean with food for them. Ralph came after me late in the afternoon and took me home, with all the dirty clothes, to our family meal. The boys were so helpful, coming home from school, getting their lessons, and helping in any way they could. Ralph was helpful also. He cooked our supper while I started washing. My washer was the old Maytag with the wringer top. I had to use two tubs for rinsing. No one had dryers then, so I had to hang the clothes out at night. If it rained, they had to be hung in the house. This was almost a daily event. Mother required many sheets and towel changes, but washing was a small part of what I wanted to do for her.

The women at Southside Baptist Church did so much for Mother and Mr. Alex. They brought food to them many times. Mother continued going to church as much as possible. The pastor, Mr. Prater, would check with Mother and plan his Sunday services to have the music worship time to be as late in the service as possible so she could get there.

Even though all Mother's family and friends were very aware of her fatal illness, life went on as normally as possible. She would be in the bed most of the day, but drag herself out and prepare for music students that she had promised to be presented in the recital soon.

Dr. Muhlendorf was faithful in his home visits to see Mother. Many times he had to wait a few minutes for her to be ready for him to see her because of her draining from her colostomy. She would always insist on his playing the piano while waiting. He played so well. I think the music helped her as much as the shot he had to give her.

So many times she would ask Willa Jean and me to go to the piano and play and sing for her. We always did what she asked. We would sing duets while tears streamed down our faces. One of her many favorites was "I don't Know Who Holds Tomorrow."

Chapter 24: Thoughts by Willa Jean 1954-55

I think I left off in 1954 when James and Mother decided for me that I would enroll in Florence State Teacher's College. Well, I did! But not under the circumstances I had thought. I never dreamed my mother would literally be on her death-bed, and I would be fulfilling one of her most desired wishes. My little girls were so helpful in helping me carry out Mother's wishes. As noted earlier, Marilyn was enrolled in Mrs. Vess's kindergarten so she walked home which was only about 4 blocks. Now I shudder when I think about letting my baby child walk that far down Almon Avenue in Tuscumbia when she was only 4 ½ years old.She told me later this was the time that she discovered that her thoughts were truly her own. No one could know what she was thinking! What a smart child I had! Mr. Alexander came by to pick Marilyn up from

kindergarten, and she spent the rest of the day with Mother. There she was entertained by Mother playing the piano or reading to her from an encyclopedia. Mother had to stay in bed part of every day by this time, so she just put Marilyn to bed with her, and they read whatever article they happened to come to when they opened the encyclopedia—presidents, polio, police, possums, etc. Marilyn loved them all. Mother let her hold her pillow and suck her thumb. She even let her eat in the bed. They had turnip greens with crackers, and Marilyn thought that was a treat! Anything that "Mammy" did was "A-ok" with my girls. The other girls were quietly making their way through the 2nd and 4th grades at Cave Street Elementary School. Later, because of Mother's health, we enrolled Marilyn in a private school on the campus of Florence State Teachers College where Celestine Butler was the teacher. She thought Marilyn was too advanced for kindergarten so she promoted her to first grade.

Many noteworthy things happened to us in Tuscumbia. Randall and JoAnne, with baby Suzanne, moved back from Mississippi and moved right next door to us. Mississippi was not for them, either. We lived directly across from the Helen Keller Home, so we were fortunate enough to see the lady herself on her last visit home. What a class act she was! And still, in the back of all these happy events, was the tragedy of Mother's illness, always looming in the background, always the first thing to think of in the morning, the last thing before going to bed. It was beginning to wear on our Mother now. She had lost quite a bit of weight and could no longer keep down her food. In spite of her poor appetite, and loss of weight, she continued teaching music. She held her last recital in late summer of 1955, just months before she died. She would get out of bed to teach her lessons, put on make-up and a big smile

Mother & her children

and just dare the rest of us to look pityingly at her. So we didn't dare! By this time, she had heard of a medicine called "Keobizim" out of Chicago which was supposed to cure cancer.

She sent for this to be taken in shot form. Of course, it was a quack! I was told this by my biology teacher Mrs. G., but she told me to let Mother use it anyway—anything to keep up her spirits! She also called me up to her desk one day and told me to "put on some make-up". I looked at her in astonishment, but she was

Mother & her grandchildren

serious. She said I was moping, which did Mother no good at all, but I should perk up and dry my eyes, hold my head up, and give Mother every bit of encouragement she could have! And so I did—except for her wishes to go to Oklahoma to be cured by Oral Roberts. We knew Mother would never be able to make the trip so we kept making excuses.

About three months before Mother's death, James and I moved to Campbell Street in Florence which was very close to the Florence Teachers College campus. The two older girls were now in the 3rd and 5th grades respectively. We were so proud of them, especially since they had had to change schools so many times, but they seemed to adjust quite well or at least we thought they did. My thoughts were still on Mother, I couldn't seem to cope with the reality of her condition--not my mother! She still played the piano so beautifully and laughed and played with the children. No one dared to mope or look sad around her. We all worked hard in preparation for her Fall recital. It was a booming success!! The children all performed beautifully and Mother looked gorgeous in her new yellow gown which was purchased at Shirley's by the parents of her music students. Her birthday was August 12 so everything was falling nicely into place. If only her health could hold up. (see picture of last recital).

Piano Recital 1955

After Mother's last recital, she seemed to lose quite a
bit of her stamina. She was still taking her Keobizim and
having Dr. Muhlendorf over for frequent visits, but the pain
was beginning to be more than she could hide, so James and
I asked her and Mr. Alex if they would move in with us so
that we could look after her a little better and she could be
closer to Sister also. They were reluctant at first, but after
talking it over, they agreed it made more sense. Sister
would not have to make the long trip to Sheffield, Mother
would be with my children during my time in classes, and
we would all be together more. James and I bought the
farm from Mother and Mr. Alex, and Mother seemed
pleased to think that it would be in the family. We drove
back up to Rogersville and looked around at her pretty

flowers, but she was too sick to get out and walk around much. Everything was beginning to be in a daze with me. I could see my mother fading fast away, and there was nothing I could do to slow the process. The doctor told us it was only a matter of time, and that we should give her all the pain medication she could endure. He came as often as possible to see her, but could do nothing except offer comfort and prayers. Our mother, who had always been our strength and comfort in time of need, now needed us to lean on. She would call out in pain during the night, not loudly, only in soft moans, but I could hear her. James was always near me, giving comfort and support. Buddy, Sister, and Robert were also there. Toward the end, we sent our children to Mama Cagle's. I think it was about this time that my emotional body gave way, along with my physical body. I was so drained of all feeling. I wanted to take the pain away from this beautiful woman who was lying here in my front bedroom. Our home was on Campbell Street, a quiet little street in North Florence which eventually runs into or close by what was the "Wildwood Park", the place where Mother penned the song which was used in the prologue of this book. This was the place she loved so much, where she and her "Dockie" had met and "courted" so many years ago.

And now James is holding her hand as she sleeps quietly, and her breath grows dimmer and dimmer. The children have all gone, and the house is quiet except for sniffles and sighs. In my mind I can hear the words "My Little Girl, I'm dreaming of you…and I'm coming home to you."

Chapter 25: Willa Jean and Lucille Together

And here is what "holds tomorrow". While our Mother is lying on her death bed in Willa Jean's front bedroom looking so beautiful and so peaceful as we dress her in one of her pretty recital gowns, all four of her "precious children" are by her side, and her "memories" are now complete. She has now left her earthly family here on Campbell Street (close to "Wildwood Park"), but we know that her family will be stronger because of her. Her legacy will live on

Mother 1955

generations after her, and her grandchildren and great-grandchildren will read about their "Mammy" with tears and laughter, and they will be better and stronger people because of her. Perhaps someday some of them will continue compiling the legacy of the "Dock and Jeannie" family tree.

Mother's children at her gravesite

Mother's grandchildren 1955

At the gravesite:
Pop, Buddy, Jo, Ralph, Sister, Mildred, Robert, Willa Jean,
James, Marilyn, Carolyn, Cathy

Epilogue

Our baby brother was the first to join Mother in death. Robert Henry died in 1991, and was followed in death by our oldest brother Buddy (Elmer Ellis) in 1996. After Mother's death, however, each of our brothers had a daughter. Robert's daughter, Jennifer Joan, was born in 1959, and Mary Jo, Buddy's daughter, was born in 1960. They completed the next generation of Dock and Jeannie Johnson's family tree.

Buddy, Willa Jean & Lucille at Daddy's grave in Knoxville.

We have never forgotten how much our mother wanted us to continue our education, and so that we

continued to do. All of Mother's grandchildren and the majority her great-grandchildren are college graduates. Mother also believed in multiplying and replenishing the earth, and that we also did. See Appendix F for the Dock Johnson Family Tree.

Mother's Grave in Florence

Yes, we're writing these lines to tell you…….

Willa Jean

I can't believe I just wrote that!

Lucille

Now where should that picture go?

Working together on
our book.

Appendices A: Father's Death

.ity's 15th Traffic Fatality—After 38 Deathless Days *Thursday - Nov. 9 1939*

Auto Death Darkens Their Future

—News-Sentinel Photo by Harold Davis

A mother, and her children who lost their father today.

An automobile made Dock Johnson Knoxville's 15th traffic fatality, and a tragic blow was dealt to the future security of these five. The children's school records are exceptional, and their father was their sole support.

Robert Henry, 9, sits on the chair arm with his mother as the five gaze into the open fire. Grouped behind, from left, are Willa Jean, 10, Mary Lucille, 13, and Elmer (Buddy), 15.

15th Traffic Victim Dies

Dock Johnson, 42, Succumbs To Hurts Received Oct. 30

Traffic death marched on Knoxville again early today when Dock Johnson, 42, of Candora Avenue, critically injured Oct. 30, died at Knoxville General Hospital—the fifteenth automobile casualty of the year.

Johnson's death at 12:30 a. m. shattered a current string of deathless holidays in the 39th day. Solemn black flags of death will fly today from the city's flagstaffs. There had been 17 deaths on city streets through the same period last year.

His death was the first since Miss Kate Simpson, 60, city school teacher, was fatally injured Sept. 30 at Magnolia Avenue and Winona Street.

Physicians at the hospital said Johnson, who has remained conscious despite severe leg and shoulder fractures and other injuries, weakened during the past few days after appearing to rally following emergency treatment.

At the time of the accident a charge of reckless driving was placed against J. A. McKee, 52-year-old Negro cook at the University of Tennessee cafeteria for more than 15 years.

McKee told Policemen Joe Edington and Earl Major that Johnson stepped in front of his automobile from the dark shadows in the 600 block of East Church Avenue and that he was unable to avoid the mishap.

Johnson, a finishing worker at Chavannes Lumber Co., and part time collector for The Knoxville Journal, is survived by his widow and four children, Elmer (Buddy) 15; Lucille, 13; Willa Jean, 11, and Robert Johnson, 9, and by nine sisters and two brothers.

'4 of Brightest Children' Lose Father in Car Death

'I Don't Know How They Can Go on,' Says Wife of Dock Johnson, 15th Traffic Victim of Year, Injured October 30.

By LEE DAVIS, *News-Sentinel Staff Writer*

Knoxville today sadly counted her 15th traffic fatality of the year and this one is particularly tragic.

Traffic death took Dock Johnson, 42, Candora Avenue, at General Hospital at 12.30 a. m., and with him it took the livelihood and future plans of "four of the brightest children in South Knoxville."

That's what teachers call the four girls and boys whom Dock Johnson leaves with the widowed mother.

"I just don't know how my children can go on without their father," said Mrs. Johnson today,—"and it wasn't his fault. I'm not even trying to think beyond the matter of the services. It is too much—that an automobile accident, over in a moment, can do this to so many lives."

Dock Johnson was struck down as he crossed the street in the 600 block of East Church Avenue just after dark on Monday, Oct. 30. J. A. McKee, 52, veteran Negro cook at University Cafeteria, has been under bond for reckless driving, charged as the driver.

Black Flags Fly Again

So for the first time in 39 days the black flags were flying again today and Knoxville had crawled up to within two of the 17 traffic dead for the same 1938 period.

And a mother and her four children had lost their sole support, the man who spent most of his waking hours working and planning for them.

Dock Johnson had completed his regular day's work in Chavannes Lumber Co. finishing department and just started on his regular night job when it happened.

Four evenings each week he left the lumber plant and trudged the streets until 9 p. m. collecting newspaper accounts.

"I always waited myself for supper with him," explained Mrs. Johnson. "He insisted on doing the two jobs. He said the children were doing so well in school that he was bound to encourage them."

Buddy, 15, is a senior at Young High and Mary Lucille, 13, is a junior there. Willa Jean, 11, is in the Eighth Grade at Vestal Grammar School, and Robert Henry, 9, is in the Fifth.

Dock Johnson was conscious to the end. He found it hard to realize what had happened to him had happened.

"Because his work took him on the streets so much he always warned all of us about watching out for automobiles," his widow said.

Warned Children

"'I always tried to watch out—I would remember how you all needed me, and to be careful,' he told me before he died.

"One of the last things Dock said to the children before they were sent out just before the end was that they must always remember to take all possible care in traffic. He said that was the least to do though even that didn't save him from an automobile.

"He had started to cross to the other side of the street. He had his pencil and notebook in his hand. Then he decided the car was coming too fast and he started back to return to the curb. He said he was trying to dodge the car when he was knocked into the air. And he came down on all the ornament things on the front and the radiator. That was how he got his worst injuries."

The driver claimed that the accident was unavoidable on his part too. He said the pedestrian was in his path in the dim street too late for him to avoid him.

Future Is Dark Now

Buddy had planned to go on to college and be a teacher-coach. He sees no possibility of that now. The problem is going to be sufficient food.

"I have a little music class," said Mrs. Johnson, "piano and voice. And that's the only work I've ever done in my life besides keeping house and caring for my four children. I don't know how to do anything else. Maybe I could learn. I'm just not going to think about it right now."

Mr. Johnson

Man Critically Injured When Hit By Auto

Dock Johnson, 42, May Not Recover

On the eve of a month free of traffic fatalities, Knoxville's safety record was threatened last night when Dock Johnson, 42, of Candora Avenue, Vestal, was critically injured when struck by a car on East Church Avenue.

Johnson, finishing worker at Chavannes Lumber Co., and part time collector for The Knoxville Journal Circulation Department, **JOHNSON** was admitted to Knoxville General Hospital with fractures of the leg and arm and severe face injuries.

It was doubtful, hospital attendants said, if he would recover. Johnson rallied after emergency surgical treatment and was termed n "fair" condition by a private physician, however.

Policemen Joe Edington and Earl Major placed a charge of reckless driving against J. A. McKee, 52, Negro, of 602 Douglas Street.

McKee, cook at the U-T cafeteria for about 15 years, told officers Johnson stepped in front of his car in the 600 block of East Church Avenue about 6 p. m.

Preliminary investigation showed that Johnson, who was collecting in the East Knoxville section for The Journal at the time, was crossing the north side of Church Avenue in about the center of the

The front of the car struck Johnson a glancing blow hurling him upon the radiator and hood of the car. A radiator ornament inflicted a deep gash on his chin and resulted in a fracture of the jaw bone.

Johnson's wife, Mrs. Jean Johnon, and their four children were t the bedside with other relatives ast night.

Mrs. Johnson explained her husband disliked inactivity and had taken the job with The Journal to occupy his time while he was working on "short hours" at the Chavannes company.

"He would spend afternoons working on the new job after leaving the mill," she explained.

The Johnson's, married 18 years this November, have two sons, imer (Buddy) Johnson, 15, and obert Johnson, 9, and two daughrs, Mary Lucille Johnson, 13, nd Willa Jean Johnson, 11.

The injured man has nine sisters, Mrs. S. M. Davis, Mrs. C. B. Ford, Mrs. Pearl Ford, Misses Grace, Elsie and Ruth Johnson, all of Knoxville, and Mrs. H. A. Burch and Mrs. Hershel Wheeler, both of Mississippi; also two brothers, Paul and E. E. Johnson, both of Knoxville.

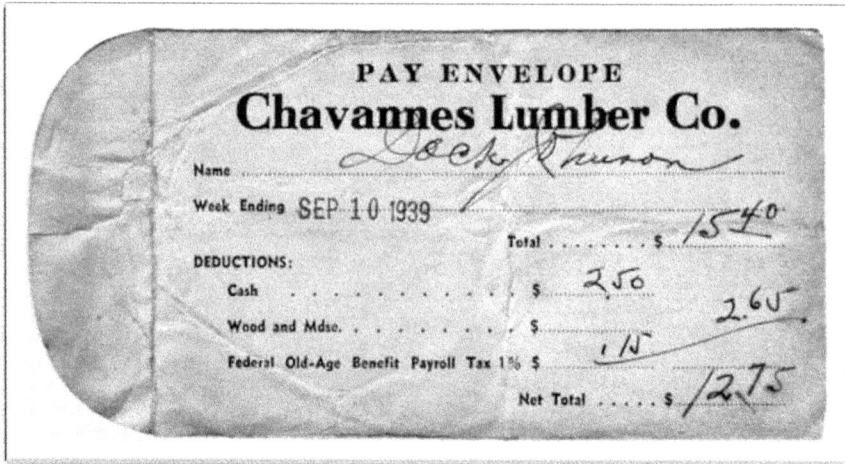

One of Daddy's last paycheck stubs

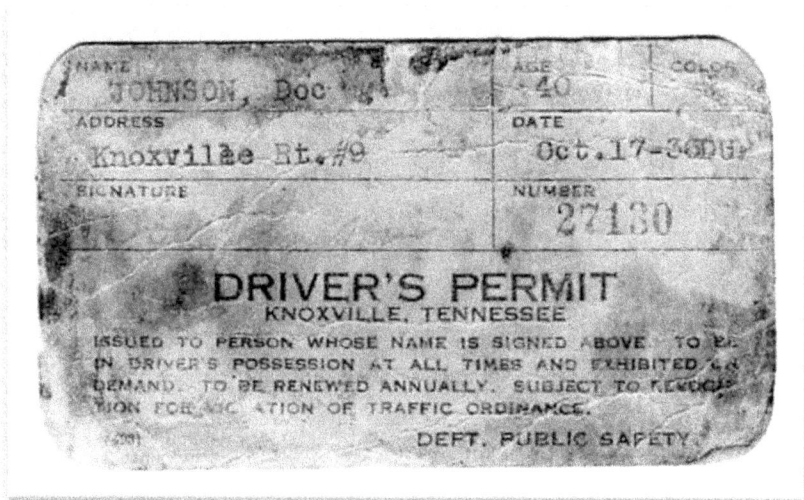

Daddy's driver's permit

Appendices B: Songs

Put My Little Shoes Away

Arr. M. Lynwood Smith

1. Moth-er dear, come bathe my forehead, I am growing very weak,
2. San - ta Claus, he gave them to me, With so man-y oth-er things,
3. Soon the ba - by will grow lar-ger, They will fit his lit-tle feet,

Let a drop of wa - - ter, Moth-er, Fall up - on my burn-ing cheek;
And I think he brought an an - gel, With a pair of gold-en wings;
Won't he look so hand-some, Moth-er, As he walks a-long the street;

Tell my lov-ing lit - tle playmates That I nev-er more shall play;
Moth-er, soon I'll be with Je - sus Ere perhaps an-oth-er day;
Moth-er, now I'll soon be leav-ing, So re-mem-ber what I say;

Give them all my toys, but moth - er,
Then, oh, then, my lov - ing moth - er, Put my lit - tle shoes a - - way.
Then, oh, then, my lov - ing moth - er,

9

197

Short'nin' Bread

TRADITIONAL

Put on de skil-let, put on de led,
Three lit-tle fel-lers ly-in' in bed,
Slipped in de kitch-en Slipped up de led
Caught wid de skil-let Caught wid de led

Mam-my's gwine to make a li'l Short-'nin' Bread Dat ain't all she's
Two was sick and toth-er most dead Sent for de doc-tor An' de
Slipped my pock-ets full of Short-'nin' Bread Stole de skil-let
Caught wid de gal mak-in' Short-'nin' Bread Paid six dollars for de skil-let. Six

gwine to do_ Mam-my's gwine to make a li'l cof-fee, too
doc-tor said_ Give dem ba-bies Short-'nin' Bread.
Stole de led_ Stole de gal to make Short-'nin' Bread
dol-lars for de led Stayed six month in jail eat-in' Short-'nin' Bread.

Mammy's lit-tle {ba-by}{fel-ler} loves short'nin' short'nin', Mammy's lit-tle {ba-by}{fel-ler} loves Short-'nin' Bread,

Mammy's lit-tle {ba-by}{fel-ler} loves short'nin' short'nin', Mammy's lit-tle {ba-by}{fel-ler} loves Short-'nin' Bread

Wait For The Wagon

R. B. BUCKLEY

Swingy

1. Will you come with me, my Phyl-lis dear, To yon blue moun-tain free? Where
   ev-'ry Sun-day morn-ing, dear, When I am by your side, We'll
2. Where the riv-er runs like sil-ver, And the birds they sing so sweet, I
   lis-ten to my sto-ry, now, It will re-lieve my heart, So

blos-soms smell the sweet-est, Come rove a-long with me. It's
jump in-to the wag-on, And all_ take a ride.
have a cab-in, Phyl-lis, And something good to eat. Come,
jump in-to the wag-on, And off_ we will start.

Chorus

Wait For The Wagon, Wait For The Wag-on, Wait For The Wag-on, And we'll all take a ride.

Robbins Music Corporation, New York, N. Y.

JEWELS.

W. O. Cushing.   Geo. F. Root.

1. When He com-eth, when He com-eth To make up His jew-els, All His
2. He will gath-er, He will gath-er The gems for His king-dom, All the
3. Lit - tle chil-dren, lit - tle chil-dren, Who love their Re-deem - er, Are the

CHORUS.

jew-els, precious jew - els, His loved and His own.
pure ones, all the bright ones, His loved and His own. Like the stars of the morning,
jew-els, precious jew - els, His loved and His own.

His bright crown a-dorn-ing, They shall shine in their beauty, Bright gems for His crown.

I Need The Prayers

J. D. V.   With feeling   James D. Vaughan

1. I need the prayers of those I love, While trav'ling o'er life's rugged way, That
2. I need the prayers of those I love, To help me in each try-ing hour, To
3. I want my friends to pray for me, To hold me up on wings of faith, That

FINE. CHORUS

I may true and faith-ful be, And live for Je-sus ev-'ry day
bear my tempted soul to Him, That He may keep me by His pow'r. I want my friends to
I may walk the narrow way, Kept by our Father's glorious grace

D. S.   I need the prayers of those I love.

pray for me, To bear my tempted soul a-bove, And in-ter-cede with God for me.

Appendices C: Marriage licenses

STATE OF TENNESSEE   LAWRENCE   COUNTY.
TO ANY MINISTER OF THE GOSPEL HAVING THE CARE OF SOULS, JEWISH RABBI, JUSTICE OF THE PEACE OF SAID COUNTY, JUDGE OR CHANCELLOR—GREETING:

You or either of you are hereby authorized to solemnize the

Rite of Matrimony

E. M. Hazelwo
Mary Lois Mason

of your County, agreeably to the direction of the Act of Assembly in such case made and provided. Provided always, that the Rite of Matrimony be solemnized in this County, otherwise this shall be null and void, and shall not be accounted any license or authority to you or either of you for the purpose aforesaid more than though the same had never been prayed or granted, etc.

Given at the Clerk's Office of said County, this
day of January 1912.

J. F. Busby

Marriage License

No. ____

E. M. Hardin

TO

Mary Lou Mason

Issued January 4th, 1902

I solemnized the Rite of Matrimony between the within parties on the 9th day of January, 1902.

R. L. R. King

Returned 14 day of Jan 1902

Recorded in Marriage:

Book M. 6, Page 153

BRANDON PRINTING CO.

STATE OF TENNESSEE, _____ COUNTY.

Personally appeared before me, J. F. Busly _____ Clerk of the County Court of said County, W. L. Hardin _____ who made oath in due form that E. M. Hardin _____ and May Lou Mason _____ are known to him and that they are each over sixteen years of age.

W. L. Hardin

Sworn to and subscribed before me, this 8 day of January 190 2

J. F. Busly _____ County Court Clerk.

_____ D. C.

The State of Alabama, Lauderdale County.

PROBATE COURT.

To any of the State Judges, or to any licensed Minister of the Gospel, or to any Justice of the Peace of said County:

KNOW YE, That you are hereby authorized and licensed to join together in the Bonds of Matrimony

Will McAnally and _Lou Mason_

Given under my hand and the seal of said Court, this the _1st_ day of _June_ , A.D. 1903.

J. J. Mitchell , Judge of Probate.

The State of Alabama, Lauderdale County.

I hereby certify that on the _1st_ day of _June_ , A.D. 1903, I solemnized the Rites of Matrimony

between _Will McAnally_ and _Lou Mason_

at _Centre Star_ , in said County.

Witness this _____ day of _____, A.D. 190_

Fifty Dollars Fine for failing to return this License.

H. E. Biggs, J. C.

The State of Alabama, Lauderdale County.

KNOW ALL MEN BY THESE PRESENTS, That we, _Will McAnally & Hardie Franklin_

are held and firmly bound unto the State of Alabama in the penal sum of *TWO HUNDRED DOLLARS* for the payment of which, well and truly to be made, we bind ourselves, and each and every of our heirs, executors, and administrators, jointly and severally, firmly by these presents.

Sealed with our seals, and dated the _1st_ day of _June_ , A.D. One Thousand Nine Hundred and _Three_

The Condition of the above Obligation is such, That, whereas, the above bound _Will McAnally_ has obtained license to intermarry and be joined in the Bonds of Matrimony with _Lou Mason_

Now, if there be no lawful cause why such marriage should not be celebrated, then this obligation to be void; otherwise to remain in full force and effect.

attest   his
Jno. L. Hughston   _Will McAnally_ (L. S.)
J. J. Mitchell   mark
                                           his
                              Hardie Franklin (L. S.)
                                           mark
                                                         (L. S.)

Taken and approved the _1st_ day of _June_ , A.D. 1903

J. J. Mitchell , Judge of Probate

The State of Alabama, Lauderdale County.

Before me, _J. J. Mitchell Judge of Probate_ in and for said County, came

personally _Will McAnally_ , who, being by me first duly and legally sworn, says, on oath, that

M _R_ is over the age of _21_ years, and appears to be over said

age, and that _Lou Mason_ is over the age of _18_ years, and appears to

be over said age, and that he makes this affidavit as to the ages of said parties for them.

attest   his
Jno. L. Hughston   _Will McAnally_
                                           mark

Sworn to and subscribed before me, this _1st_ day of _June_ , 1903.

J. J. Mitchell , Judge of Probate.

Marriage License 1c, Lauderdale County.

MARRIAGE RECORD
LAUDERDALE COUNTY, ALABAMA

Dock Johnson and _Fannie J. Woodware_

THE STATE OF ALABAMA, LAUDERDALE COUNTY

TO ANY MINISTER OF THE GOSPEL, JUDGE OF THE SUPREME OR CIRCUIT COURTS, OR CHANCELLOR OF SAID STATE, JUDGE OF PROBATE, OR ANY JUSTICE OF THE PEACE OF SAID COUNTY—GREETING:

You are hereby authorized to celebrate the Rite of Matrimony between _Dock Johnson_

(white—black) and _Fannie J. Woodware_ and this shall be your sufficient authority for so doing.

Given under my hand and seal, this _11_ day of _Nov._ 192 _7_ _J. J. Howne_

Judge of Probate

THE STATE OF ALABAMA, LAUDERDALE COUNTY

The above named parties were married by me at _Ingrams Cross Roads_ on the _12th_ day of _Nov._ 192 _7_

F. A. Glover

Minister of the Gospel

THE STATE OF ALABAMA, LAUDERDALE COUNTY

KNOW ALL MEN BY THESE PRESENTS, That we .... are held and firmly bound unto the State of Alabama, in the penal sum of Two Hundred Dollars, for the payment of which, well and truly to be made, we bind ourselves, and each and every one of our heirs, executors, and administrators, jointly and severally, firmly by these presents.

Sealed with our seals and dated at Florence, Alabama, the .... day of .... A.D. One Thousand Nine Hundred and ....

The Condition of the Above Obligation is Such, That, whereas, the above bound .... has obtained License to intermarry and be joined in the Bonds of Matrimony with ....

Now, if there be no lawful cause why such marriage should not be solemnized, then this obligation to be void; otherwise to remain in full force and effect.

.... (L. S.)

.... (L. S.)

Taken and approved the .... day of .... 192 .... (L. S.)

Judge of Probate

THE STATE OF ALABAMA, LAUDERDALE COUNTY.

AFFIDAVIT AS TO AGE OF PARTIES

Before me, _Fannie Woodware, Notary_ Judge of Probate in and for said County, came personally .... who, being by me first duly and legally sworn, says, on oath, that

M _Dock Johnson_ is over the age of _21_ years, and that

M _Fannie J. Woodware_ is over the age of _18_ years, and that he makes this affidavit as to the ages of said parties for them.

Dock Johnson

Sworn to and subscribed before me, this _11_ day of _Nov._ 192 _7_

Fannie Woodware

Notary Public

Appendices D: Letters and Poems

205

The following are birthday poems from the battle front,
1943, to his sisters in October and November:

October 19, 43

My Dear [sister]

*As it's nearing your sixteenth
birthday I feel it my duty
and pleasure to write you
a letter showing my most
devoted love for you and
remembrance of the occasion.
I sincerely hope you have
a very happy birthday and
many, many happy returns.
So I close this letter
wishing you again a very
'HAPPY BIRTHDAY' and
sending my everlasting love*

your brother
[signature]

To Will & Jean

I dream of Jeanie with the Raven
   hair,
Borne like a vapor on the golden
   air,
I see her tripping where the
   bright stream plays
As gay as the daisies along
   her way.
I hear her voicing melodies as
   tuneful as love,
Warm as the sunlighting
   heaven above.

       yours etc —
        E.F.

"To MARY"

M is for the million things
   She's done for me.
A is for the everlasting love
   and admiration I have for her.
R is for the reality of
   that love.
Y is for the happy years
   we've spent together.
   Put them all together
   and they spell Mary
   a girl whom I adore
   with all my heart.

                    Buddy

From Buddy to his sister in response to her marriage
announcement.

Postcard to sister announcing Willa Jean's Wedding to
James.

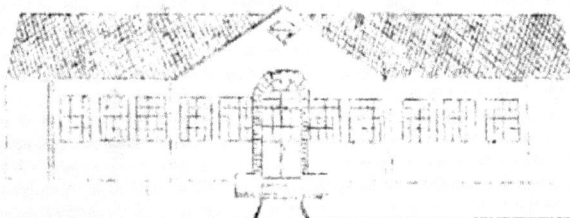

ANDERSON SCHOOL NEWS

VOL NO. I KNOXVILLE, TENN. NOV 23, 1936 ISSUE NO I

ON TO THE CARNIVAL

With the aid of the students and the cooperation of the parents, steps are being taken toward a coronation festival. We are taking two representatives from each class, starting from the fourth through the eighth grade. Each penny counts one vote. The girl getting the most votes is to be crowned queen of the Carnival, and the boy getting the largest amount will be elected king. He will crown the queen.

The representatives who were nominated for queen and king who are not elected will be candidates and each receive a prize

The Coronation scene will follow a short "Black Face Comedy", given by the students. Let's all be here for a great evening of entertainment. ADMISSION 10 cents.

NOMINEES FOR KING AND QUEEN

Fourth	Beatrice Williams Robert Webb
Fifth	C. E. Renaw Imogene Ford
Sixth	Willie McClain Louise Webb
Seventh	Roy Ford Nell Cobble
Eighth	Jack Clapp Mildred Maples

READ MR. REED'S ARTICLE ON "PHYSICAL EDUCATION IN THE FUTURE" BOTTOM OF PAGE NUMBER THREE

ON TO THE CARNIVAL

-POETS CORNER-

THANKSGIVING

We all like Thanksgiving, I know
   that much,
But sometimes people on holidays
   just have to fuss,
Most of the time it is when we
   are away from school,
Because then we don't have to
   mind the teachers' rule.

But most of all we like the
   feast,
Which mother prepares for us
   to eat,
With pies and cake and pudding,
   she bakes,
And candy so sweet that children help make.

On Thanksgiving morn, when children awake,
They should arise with a smiling
   face,
And try to think of some good
   deed,
To help someone in direst need.

We sh all be thankful for our
   heal.
And re . . . r Thanksgiving through
   all wealth,
We should make others happy and
   be happy too,
And not forget to thank our God
   the whole day through.

            By Mary Lucile Johnson

Poem by Lucille - 1938

A. R. PEDIGO--------PASTOR.
314 Ogle St. --'Phone 2-0791.
DECEMBER 25, 1938.
' ' ' ' ' ' ' ' ' ' ' ' '
MORNING SERVICE.

Prelude
Hymn--Joy to the World------------------- 17
Announcements
Offering
XMAS. PRO. BY THE CHILDREN.

Hymn--Oh, Come all Ye Faithful--Congregation
Recitation--Dear Friends-----------Jean Burns
Recitation---Pictures-------------Betty Souls
Recitation---Mother's Treasure---C. L. Huling
Recitation---The Gifts we may bring
                         Johnny Ruth Moore
Hymn--Luther's Cradle Song-----------Jr. Choir
Recitation-The Mouse's share----Wendal Atchley
Recitation--The Children's King---Ila Atchley
Reading--Hello Santa Claus-Willie Jean Johnson
Recitation--Little Baby Jesus----Wayne Nelson
Recitation-----------------------Mary Jane Ford
Hymn--Silent Night---------Johnson Quartette.
Recitation---Our Guide-------------Leon Nelson
Recitation---The Xmas. Story--------Dewey Lee
Reading---The Reason Why-----Dorothy Wallace.
Hymn--Oh, Little Town of Bethlehem-Jr. Choir.
Recitation--"Peace"------------Five Children.
Recitation--If Santa was my Pa--Buddy Thomas.
Recitation------------Beverly Ann Bodenheimer
Hymn-It Came upon a Midnight Clear-Jr. Choir.
Recitation--Today the Prince of Peace is born
                         --Jo Ann LaRew
Recitation---A little Tot--Anna Lee Tomlinson
Recitation---For Mother--------Thomas Lindsay
Recitation---A Little Babe-----Lois Pridemore
Recitation---Merry Xmas.-----Evelyn Pridemore

' ' ' ' ' ' ' ' ' ' ' ' ' '
Training Union 6:15

This is a typed interpretation of the letter on the following page.

Florence, Ala
Star Route 5
Oct 10, 1938

Monday morn –
Dear Jean – Will write you again and let you know how we are. Jean, do hope you all are well, but now listen – here comes the news – take it easy – Don't go worry if you can help it. I hate so bad to tell you but I got to – me and your dada went to town Saturday and spent most all day having a good time together, just me and him and was on our way back and right in town the man we was riding with run too close to a large truck and your dada had his arm out the door and it broke his arm all in pieces. We rushed him wright on to the hospital and Dr. Jackson taken it off wright above his elbow. I thought he would bleed to death before the doctor come. Jean, I never could live at all---He begged for us all to tell Walter not to live like he had. See he had to die and he was not ready – Oh, just everything – I was alone by myself......??? They made us leave??? We went back Sunday. Stayed most of the day. We have a real nice box. And we put your dada's arm in it. Wrapped it in a half-sheet and carried it to Jones Hill Graveyard and buried it. There was a large???Just like a real "berring" it liked to killed everyone of us. I stayed with your dada at the hospital and the children went and buried his arm. Everyone was got??to see it up there and we wrote what arm it was and sealed it inside of a quart fruit jar and sit it at the head of his arm. I thought that was right for it was part of your dada's body, Jean. Your dada is doing fine. Doctor said guess he could be brought home...oh law..your dada will mis his wright arm the rest of his days. WC said ah papa has worked long enough for us now we work for him. Jean don't worry we do all that can be done for him. The man from Letan Alabama had a large seed truck parked way out in the middle of the street....(not legible)...
... Pickwick Dam at $1.00 per hour and still lives at Pine Ridge. The children are all well. They start to school Monday morning. Your dada cut hay all last week......
...Tell the children he looks good all but he lost his wright arm. I write often I would have sent for you but the doctor said he would be all right if he would live through the week. I close. Love to all. Your mother

Florence Colo
Star Route 5
Oct 10 1938

Monday morn
Dear gang ~ (Will write)
going to let you knoll that we
is again & hope you all is well
let yall lisume there comes the
news. take it easey & te git
warry if you can help it I
hate So Boy I tell you let I
got time to go your Dodo was
I talkin with my She &
~~Hagen~~ talken and ~~ham~~
d good time to go ather j it was
and her ~~~~ & Wat am his way
Back ~~~~ I Write in tallin thy
now We Wet rideing with
rin & clase to a large
truck and jer dodo had
his Arm out the Daar
~~and it~~ Broke his Ar
~~in Broke~~ We ~~riddeg~~ her
write ~~~~ & the hospitl
and Dr dockersam tok
it off Write a bote his

...d the child...
Berved his din... ...
...it & See it...
Whate what mu...
...d the...
...at a...
...it at her of his...
thought that what write for
it is a Sort of your doest
Body your... your dada i...
Dofing fine Dr Seed ge...
he ca... Bee Brought fr...
the la...
nothing... & ah hall...
dada tirkel was his Wright
din the rest...
Wesend at Pipo that...
long enough... I... for...
nail the work for her...
Don't Worry We Do all that
can be Done for her. the
...
...large Doo...
...Parked Way at i...
middle of the Street

e that snowed
the children got sick ... let the
was care Every tale
... and ... til ...
that Effie might tel say
let Effie that Photo ... ...
... ... Dr ... ...
... ... all Well we
Still Working Effie gone back
to Pick Wick Dam at 10 per hour
E. Bill lives at Pine Ridge ...
children is all Well they start
to School monday when
... did hay ... last Week
he got some ... & go ...
... ...
... hay well ... ...
... Dr Who ... hospital ... I will
haf he is I be glad When he
can come home tell the
children he forget going all
let he last his Wright Drink
you Write ... I Would of
... for you let Dr Say he
get all Wrts ... we y have
had ... ... Weeks I close
love to all your mother

Florence Ala
Oct 17 - 1938
Monday morn
Dear ____ and family Will
write you again & let you
know all that We is We Brought
our dada home this day night
from the hospital he doying
Very Well he walket a long
he got & go & the Dr a
gain & Day. he has got
Every other Day he Send tell
you his drug was hurting
him a lot this ____
S. & Bill come Sunday
Stayed all Day Bill is
working at PickWick dam
gets $1.00 Per hour - & Still
lives at Pine Ridge
Darline gean is on the
Kender gorden Billy & Met
& Mcclen high & Toy
with rest of the children
he & yes coll ____ & go
So & fixed her Sweet &
let her, & ____

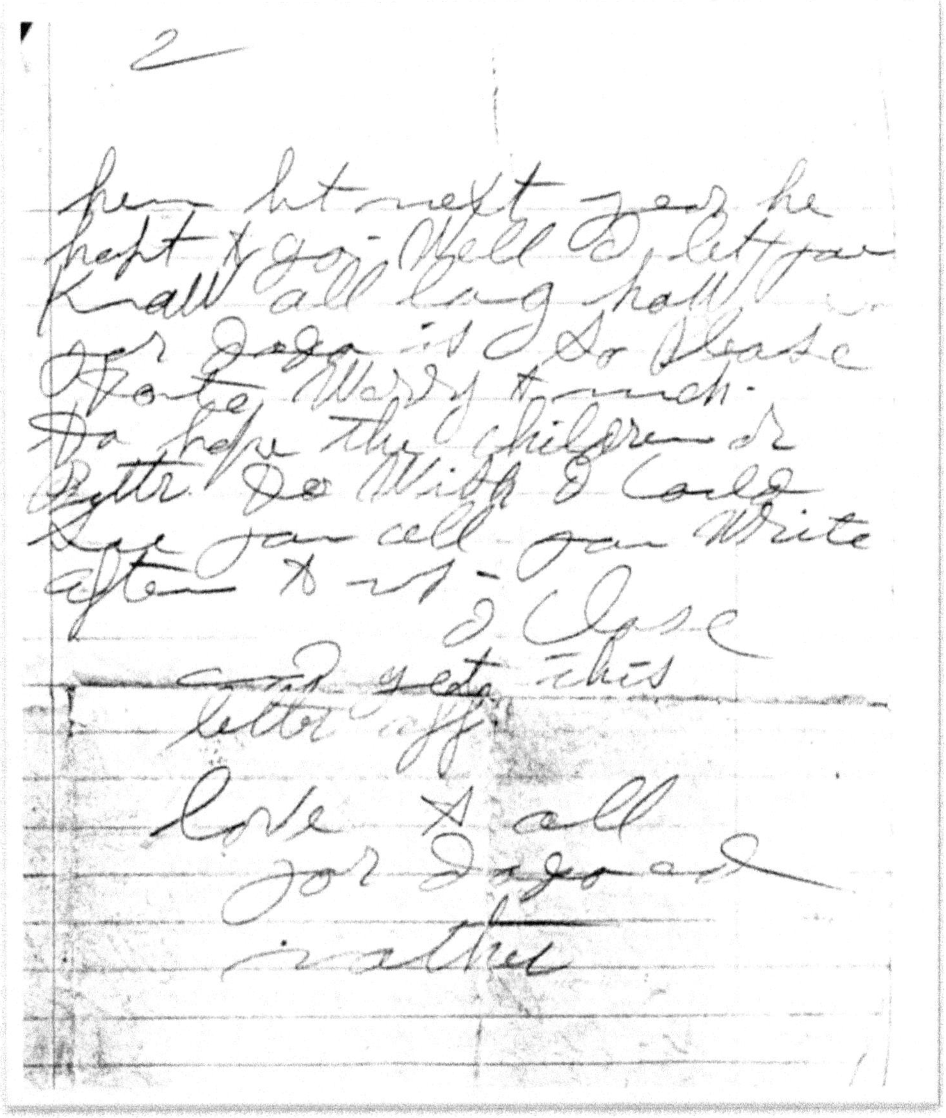

here but next year he
hopt to go. Well I let you
Know all I can hall
your dada is so please
Forgive Merry to much.
So hope the children is
Better So Wish I could
See you all you write
after X-m. I close
and get this
letter off
love to all
your dada and
mother

Florence ala-
march 20 1938
Sunday night at home
Dear gean and Joely Rec jor letter glad
you is all Well So sorry Boddie got hurt
So hope he be careful and donte get hurt
We is all up I feel Blue & & Day had a
Bad Day. rest is Well I hove to much
Worry thats Whats Wrong. for one thing
I Cyed nast all Day. gean We got the
house Wired We got 6 lights in 6 Rooms
and one Porch light and a Back ligh
at We Will Soon get the Porch Builet
on the Back Do With jor Mat Mede
Beatrice Bought a $100 one Hardore
Dallor Raido I mean its a 1938 Sre
is Pretty We get Knoxville and
Nary Where its nearly height at my
hood I sit off till I get Sleepy then
a turn it off and go to bed I get
Preaching every norn. I heard
jor ncle Daniel & Bayet Sing t
Day Nr the Raido a 3 clack at
Sheffield ala. I mean it Wot good
t gean Joe Sledge Died last
Week. Dont like Nary any Mr Kuell
is all nast Done gone gett it if Day

time soon I don't think I just would
be glad Seems like the children
& all so jellas of each other they
should not life that way for I love
you all and would do any thing I
could for any of you all Sometimes
I think they would be glad & get
me out of the way so they could
do as they please but I am the
only thing that is keeping this bunch
together I see thats the gest that
why I an here Bee called Virginia &
talkin and gave her a nice present
She lookt good gean I got lots
& sure do with I could tell you
but cant write it my helth is
able Bod- I up those you dodo are
past drink lats I just beg all time
for hem & see and I quit gean he
has lats & warry over seems
like they all look & hem see and
thats warry do hope you will come
home that summer at it would
be the first time in your life
you could relly call it your own
home and a Pretty one & and well
fixed in house

Mrs Dock. Johnson
Vestel Ave.
Condato Road
Rov. 23.
Knoxville Tenn.

Appendices E: Dykes Cherokee Indian Heritage

Jim Dykes plans to hike Cherokees' Trail of Tears

By The Associated Press

Jim Dykes has hog-tied wild boars and used dogs to hunt bears. He's also raised five kids and edited the Tennessee Valley Authority's award-winning newspaper, Inside TVA.

Now Dykes, at 51, plans to become the first person to voluntarily walk the Cherokees' infamous Trail of Tears.

Dykes, a Rockford resident and former writer at The Daily Times, has been given a leave of absence from TVA to hike the trail from Red Clay near Cleveland, Tenn., to Tahlequah, Okla., beginning Dec. 17. In exchange for the unpaid leave, he has agreed to return to TVA all of his notes, stories, photographs and memorabilia picked up along the way.

The National Park Service, which ran out of money before fulfilling a congressional mandate to document the Trail of Tears, has encouraged the project. So have the Cherokees and TVA's own historians.

When he first thought of the project 20 years ago, Dykes said, he wanted to do it for his own personal satisfaction.

"And then I thought, 'Face reality, kid. You write for a living, and you will write stories about this,' " Dykes said a telephone conversation from his Knoxville office. "Then I started thinking about how to do it.

"Then the kids got bigger and got into their teen-age stuff and I couldn't think about anything except how to keep the little creeps out of jail and myself from going crazy," said Dykes, a memorable 6-foot-2, 250-pounder with eyebrows shaped like Swiss roofs. "But they're essentially grown now, and my wife, Peg, is with me 100 percent."

TVA was more difficult to convince, until Dykes persuaded the agency that his walk would help the National Park Service, the Cherokees, TVA and anyone interested in the history of the Tennessee Valley.

"But the project has turned into what I've been doing for 20 years — a damn street reporter — walking around, getting the story. It's going to be a lot of work. But it will also be a great and glorious adventure and it should bring me honor in the tribe," said Dykes, who inherited Cherokee blood from his mother and father.

The Cherokees were removed from their ancestral homes in Tennessee, North Carolina and northern Georgia during the 1830s. Fifteen thousand Cherokees started the forced march to Oklahoma in 1838; 4,000 died along the way. The route of the walk through Tennessee, Kentucky, Illinois, Missouri, Arkansas and Oklahoma, became known as the Trail of Tears.

"Nobody knows exactly where it is. I expect I'll find people along the way who know where a part of the trail is. I'll find graves and I'll find markers," Dykes said.

He doesn't plan to walk through cities. Dykes said he'll hike through the woods and follow old wagon roads, charting each step and toting a light pack, bedroll and tent.

Is he scared?

"Yes. I'd be a damn fool if I weren't. Those blizzards and things get pretty bad out there. And I'll be lonely and discouraged, I'm sure," he said.

"I think I'll be finding quite a few people along the way who have Cherokee roots in their past. Most people in Tennessee have a sympathy for the Indians who were driven out by Jackson and the Army. The people who live along the trail take a proprietary interest, and those stories and legends have been passed down."

He also plans to write a book about it, and along the way he'll file stories with newspapers in Tennessee, Georgia, Oklahoma and Missouri.

"One word will take care of why I'm doing this — glory," Dykes said. "How many people do you know who can say they do what they do for the glory?"

Jim was my mother's Cousin - Uncle Joe Dykes son. a reporter for the Knoxville paper.

223

Columnist Dykes to hit Trail of Tears

BY TERRI WEINTRAUB
Journal Reporter

As a reporter, Jim Dykes was known for his unconventional behavior.

His antics included running a federal beat from a tavern and asking a beauty queen if she had ever run over a dog and, if so, what did it feel like.

But the feat that will bestow national recognition on Dykes, 51, a Knoxville Journal columnist and editor of Inside TVA, will be his planned hike across the Cherokee Indians' 1,200-mile Trail of Tears.

The hike, to document the trail over which the Cherokees traveled to Oklahoma after being forced from their land in the 1830s, is expected to begin Dec. 17 from Red Clay, near Cleveland, and finish in Tahlequah, Okla., March 26.

"It ain't going to last no 40 damn years, like some other people I know," Dykes said in a joking reference to the Hebrew wandering.

See Dykes, Page A11

Jim Dykes: looking forward to 1,200-mile trek.

in the desert with Moses en route to the promised land.

Humor aside, the father of five and grandfather of two who got a leave of absense from TVA for the project, said he is nervous about the journey through rugged terrain in the merciless winter. Of the 15,000 Cherokees who started the involuntary march from their ancestral homes, 4,000 died along the way.

"I'll be worried about hypothermia and staggering around silly," said Dykes, who has pointed, bushy eyebrows like former Soviet leader Leonid Brezhnev.

With a backpack, sleeping bag and tent, Dykes said he plans to camp most of the time, switching to a motel when his wife, Peg, meets him on the weekends she can find him.

Dykes said he plans to write a book about his journey, as well as file stories with newspapers along the route in Tennessee, Georgia, Oklahoma and Missouri.

Some of the the journey will be on old wagon roads nobody has documented, Dykes said.

"But the county historians and the natives will know," he said.

"Walking I'll be able to take notes and I'll have a map and I'll be able to mark it all.

"I've always been lucky and run into people who told me the right things and got stories.

"And when I come out in Tahlequah, I'll have a string of notes and maps nobody will have."

Dykes said he plans to turn over his collection of information to TVA. And, he said, the National Park Service can use it to dedicate a national historic trail.

The park service began to document the trail under a congressional mandate but it ran out of funds and never completed the project.

Dykes, who is part Cherokee himself, said he has been wanting to make this journey for more than 20 years.

Now, with his children grown and "a job good enough to leave the money from," he said he can fulfill "my own private dream."

"As I said in my column, it'll be a great adventure, if I don't freeze my ass off or get run over by a beer truck," he said.

Dykes, whose column about the people and places and culture in East Tennessee has produced somewhat of a cult following, said he hasn't been preparing much for his upcoming task.

"I got a leave and I'm having a party — lots of parties," he said.

Appendices F: Family Tree

Family Tree of William Cooley Ellis Johnson and Jeannie Veandra
Mahatha Elmer Ellis Reece Johnson Family

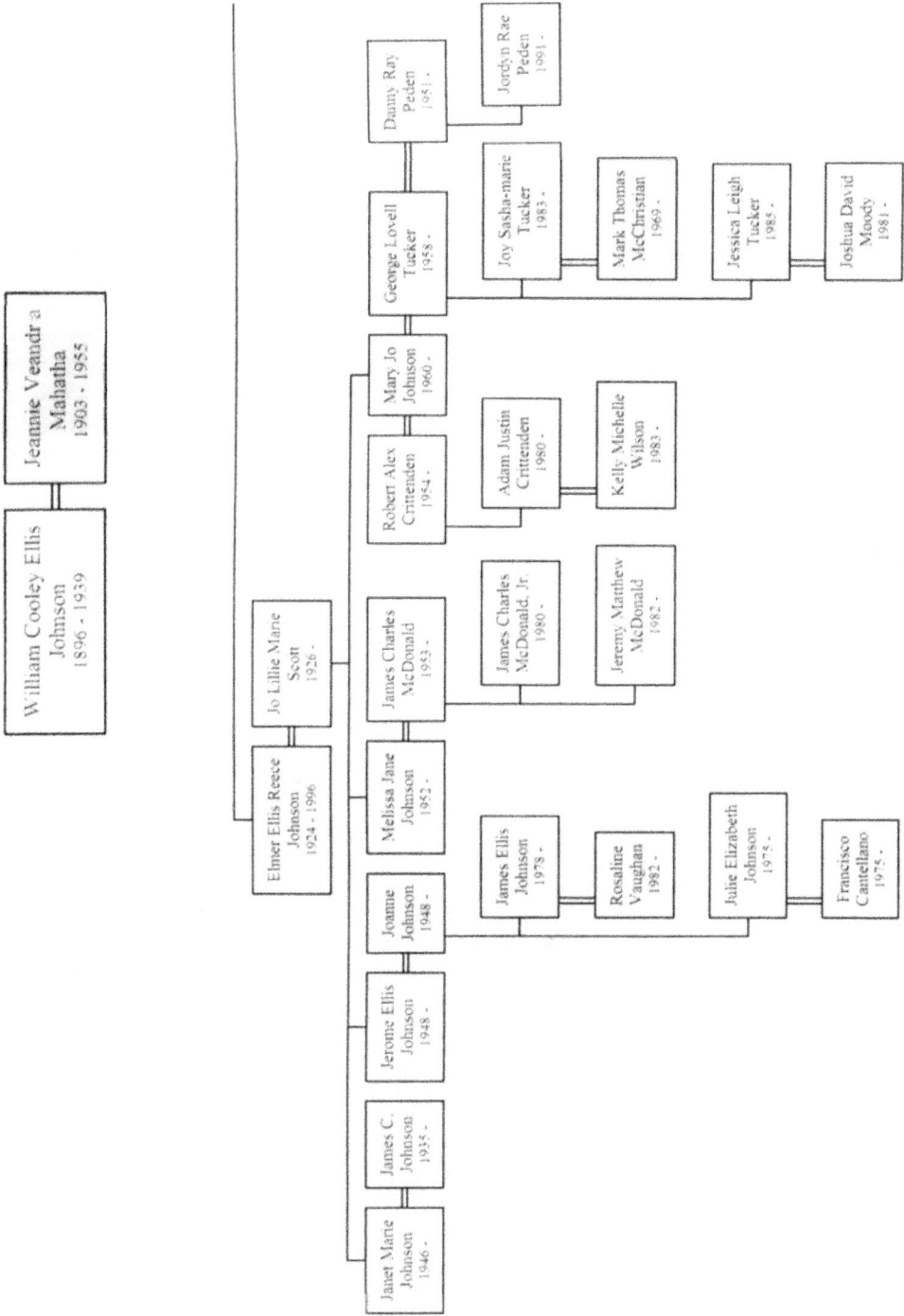

William Cooley Ellis Johnson 1896 - 1939

Jeannie Veandra Mahatha 1903 - 1955

Elmer Ellis Reece Johnson 1924 - 1996

Jo Lillie Marie Scott 1926 -

Janet Marie Johnson 1946 -

James C. Johnson 1938 -

Jerome Ellis Johnson 1948 -

Jeanne Johnson 1948 -

Melissa Jane Johnson 1952 -

James Charles McDonald 1953 -

Mary Jo Johnson 1960 -

George Lovell Tucker 1958 -

Danny Ray Peden 1951 -

Jordyn Rae Peden 1991 -

Joy Sasha-marie Tucker 1983 -

Mark Thomas McChristian 1960 -

Jessica Leigh Tucker 1985 -

Joshua David Moody 1981 -

Robert Alex Crittenden 1954 -

Adam Justin Crittenden 1980 -

Kelly Michelle Wilson 1983 -

James Charles McDonald. Jr. 1980 -

Jeremy Matthew McDonald 1982 -

James Ellis Johnson 1978 -

Rosaline Vaughan 1982 -

Julie Elizabeth Johnson 1975 -

Francisco Castellano 1975 -

227

Family Tree of William Cooley Ellis Johnson and Jeannie Veandra Mahatha Mary Lucille Johnson, Willa Jean Johnson and Robert Henry Johnson Families

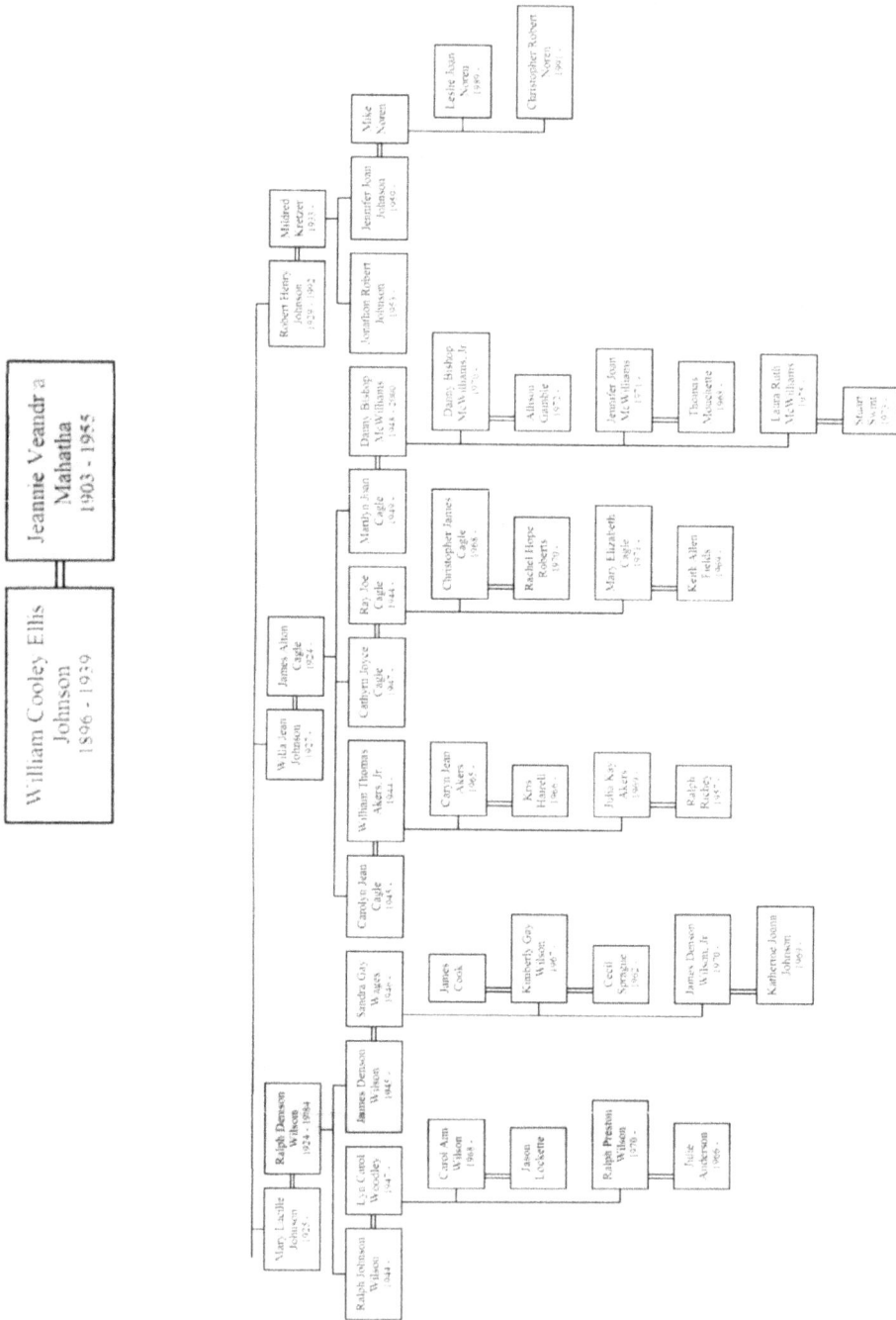

Bluewater Publications is a multi-faceted publishing company capable of meeting all of your reading and publishing needs. Our two-fold aim is to:
1) Provide the market with educationally enlightening and inspiring research and reading materials and to
2) Make the opportunity of being published available to any author and or researcher who so desires to become published.

We are passionate about preserving history; whether it is through the re-publishing of an out-of-print classic, like the one you just read, or by publishing the research of historians and genealogists; Bluewater Publications is the peoples' choice publisher.

For company information or for information about how you can be published through Bluewater Publications, please visit:

www.BluewaterPublications.com

Confidently Preserving Our Past,
Angela Broyles and Crystal Broyles
Bluewater Publications.com
Formerly Known as Heart of Dixie Publishing

www.ingramcontent.com/pod-product-compliance
Lightning Source LLC
Chambersburg PA
CBHW061830260326
41914CB00005B/944